THE NAGA RESISTANCE MOVEMENT

Prospects of Peace and Armed conflict

Dr. Aosenba

2016

Regency Publication

A Division of

Astral International Pvt. Ltd.

New Delhi - 110 002

First Published, 2001
Reprinted, 2016

ISBN: 978-81-87498-37-7 (Hardbound)

Publisher's note:

Every possible effort has been made to ensure that the information contained in this book is accurate at the time of going to press, and the publisher and author cannot accept responsibility for any errors or omissions, however caused. No responsibility for loss or damage occasioned to any person acting, or refraining from action, as a result of the material in this publication can be accepted by the editor, the publisher or the author. The Publisher is not associated with any product or vendor mentioned in the book. The contents of this work are intended to further general scientific research, understanding and discussion only. Readers should consult with a specialist where appropriate.

Every effort has been made to trace the owners of copyright material used in this book, if any. The author and the publisher will be grateful for any omission brought to their notice for acknowledgement in the future editions of the book.

Published by : **Regency Publication**
A Division of
Astral International Pvt. Ltd.
– ISO 9001:2008 Certified Company –
4760-61/23, Ansari Road, Darya Ganj
New Delhi-110 002
Ph. 011-43549197, 23278134
E-mail: info@astralint.com
Website: www.astralint.com

Digitally Printed at : **Replika Press Pvt. Ltd.**

PRINTED IN INDIA

Preface

The book is an attempt to explore why the Nagas ethnopolitical movement has endured over the last five decades after India's Independence. What are the dynamics of Naga ethnopolitical movement. What role does the leadership play and what are the possibilities of internationalisation of Naga issue, its external implications and prospects for management of the problem. Eventually a solution is discussed in the following chapters, based on the theoretical premises laid by various experts, analyst in their respective fields.

This book deals with the Naga resistance movement with its national and international dimensions. The study is a contribution to the fields of security/strategic and peace studies apart from touching on problems of modernisation and stabilisation in the developing countries. It has involved a selective use of historical materials some of which are only available in London (UK). It was necessary to condense a large amount of material which included unpublished source material. The book is relevant to contemporary problems faced by Naga political society and policy questions facing the underground Nagas and the Government of India.

The study grew out of my experience as a Naga who is deeply concerned with the reality around us and is constantly looking for various alternative strategies to reverse the trends of war and violence.

My research strategy for the Naga problems involved a mixture of theoretical and empirical approaches. To cover both the historical development of the Naga Ethnic movement and the later Naga Resistance Movement. In addition I have concentrated on analysis at the individual level on Phizo as an ideologue and policy maker. It is important to understand

Phizo's world view and value system and especially his "peace ideas". Those studies which have ignored Phizo or underestimated the importance of his legacy, can only produce a distorted image of Naga reality. An individual's personality can be a source of perception for misperception depending upon how functional the individual's cognitive map is in a given situation.

The central argument of this study is that the Indo-Naga conflict with its bloodshed, military patrols and encounters and human rights violations can give way to an era of peace and prosperity if the discourse of domination and militarisation is replaced by the creation and projection of images of peace and differences are dealt with "by designing a problem solving process that promotes new thinking of long standing problems. I list below the currently perceived choices that flow from the central argument.

1. The uniqueness of the historical situation of the Nagas in relation to India. Nagaland was part of the British Empire but not, strictly speaking, of India.
2. Developments around the independence of India: Naga declaration of Independence the day before India declaration, Mahatma Gandhi said the Nagas should only join the Union if they wished to do so voluntarily.
3. The armed conflict which no side could win.
4. Need to abandon old stands from both sides: creative solutions must be sought that satisfy the needs and aspirations of the Naga people and the vital interests of India, especially its security needs.
5. Emphasise that the situation is a unique one, not comparable to other insurgency conflicts faced by India. There should be no implication that any agreement which may be reached with Naga leaders would have repercussions for negotiations with other insurgency movement.
6. I believe at this stage no particular solution should be presented (as this could prejudice the negotiations themselves).
7. Everywhere in the world statemen/women are being praised for their willingness to negotiate with movement with whom their Governments have been at war. In many

cases decades' old conflicts have been resolved around the negotiating table. Making peace, for which making important concessions is imperative, is today seen as an act of great statesmenship. It strengthens the position of a government: the fear making concessions, even major one, weaken the position of a government has been proved wrong again and again.

8. The government has the strength to negotiate a mutually acceptable dealt; let it have the foresight to fully utilise the opportunity that is now presented to talk to the NSCN with an open mind, fairness, and a sincere commitment to achieve a lasting and just peace which will strengthen India and strengthen the Nagas.

Contents

Acknowledgements

I am highly indebted to Professor M.L. Sondhi, Chairman, Indian Council of Social Science Research (ICSSR) New Delhi, Dr. Ajai Sahni, Executive Director, South Asia Terrorism Portal, New Delhi, for suggestion, inspiration and guidance.

I am equally grateful to my friends Mr. & Mrs. Alem Jamir for correcting my manuscript, and to Dr. Lanu, Dr. Rajan, Biplove, Somu, Druba, Gideon, Pao, Kovi, Lima and Robin for their help and suggestions.

I also take this opportunity to thank the entire library staff of JNU Nehru Memorial Library, Institute for Strategic Analysis and also the British Library, London, Oriental and Indian Office Library London for excellent facility.

I am very indebted to Apok Jamir for the financial support which has been of great help.

Finally I owe debt of gratitude to my parents, brother and sister whose love and prayer for me remained as a constant source of inspiration and encouragement.

New Delhi Dr. Aosenba
Date: 30 July, 2001

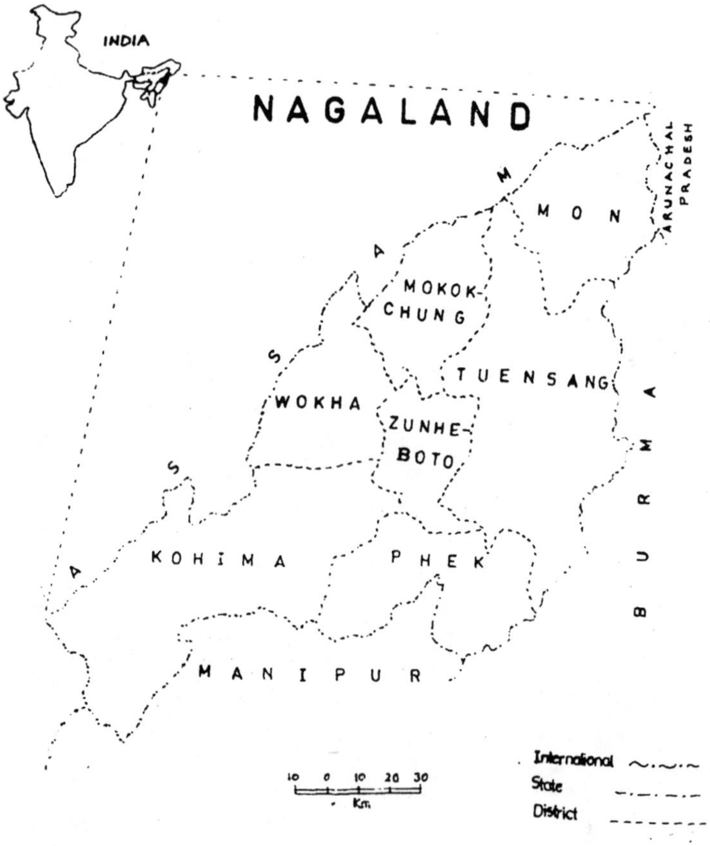

Source: 1991 Census Yearbook, Director of Census,
Government of India

CHAPTER ONE

Land and the People: A Brief History

The Nagas who are presently settled in the hill region of the tri-junction of India, Burma (Myanmar) and China have occupied the region called the Naga hills for centuries. There are various theories about the origin and how and why they have been called the Nagas. It is generally assumed that the plethora of tribes who are called Nagas have something in common with each other which distinguishes them from the many other people and tribes found in Assam.[1] However the origin of the term Naga and its people are as mysterious as any theory of origin of any race or community in the history.

The term 'Naga' includes the various tribes who have spread across the present states of Nagaland, Manipur, Arunachal Pradesh, Assam and some parts of Myanmar (Burma). The total Naga population in Indo-Myanmar is estimated at "not less than two million and they are scattered over a contiguous region starting from the Brahmaputra valley in Assam in the west, to the Chindwin river in north-west Burma in the east, most Manipur in the south and Tirap and Changlang district in Arunachal Pradesh to the north."[2]

According to J.P. Mills, "The Naga inhabited areas are bounded by the Hukawang valley in the north-east, the plains of the Brahmaputra valley to the north-west of Cachar to the south-west and of the Chindwin to the East. In the south the Manipur valley roughly marks the point of contact between the 'Naga tribes' and the very much closely inter-related group of Kuki tribe."[3] For hundreds of years, "The Naga tribes remained untouched by higher civilization, neither Hindu culture nor the influence of Buddhism into these hills, where primitive races were persisting in ancient types of culture."[4]

A. Origin of the Word 'Naga'

Before the advent of the British into the Naga Hills, the inhabitants of these hills knew themselves by the designation of their respective tribes only. The name however was not in general use among the Nagas. It was in the last century after the occupation of some parts of the particular hill range, that the British colonialist called the hill areas as Naga Hills, then onwards the term 'Naga' began to be widely used for all these tribes who settled in this range.

There are various theories about the origin of the word 'Naga' and there is no unanimity of the opinion. Inspite of the different theories regarding the origin of the term 'Naga' however there is a consensus that the word 'Naga' is given to particular tribes by the Aryan speaking people to mean naked hill people. It is a fact that the word 'Naga' remained a terror to the Aryan speaking Assamese for ages. To them it was understood to mean naked 'Hill Men of head Hunter."[5]

Ptolemy, the Greek scholar in his *Geographia* had mentioned the words 'Naga log' which means the realm of the naked people[6] in about 150 A.D. Interestingly, the location which Ptolemy described about the naked people has been the exact place in which the present Nagas are living now.

Another theory is that the word 'Naga' originated from the word 'Nag' meaning 'snake' in general and the 'cobra' in particular. But this is usually referred to the snake worshipper, which is prevalent in many parts of India,[7] but such worshippers are not called the Nagas. This theory has no significance to the Naga of the Northeast India, because Nagas were never worshippers of snakes.

Further theory attributed to J.H. Hutton suggests that the word 'Naga' originally was a corruption of the Assamese word 'Noga' (pronounced Naga) probably meaning a "mountaineer"[8] It is merely a European lengthening of Assamese word Noga (Pronounced Naga).

According to Captain Butler, "the term Naga is derived from the Bengali word 'Nangla' or the Hindustani word 'Naga' meaning 'naked', crude and barbarous, while another theory suggests that the Cachar word Naga 'a youngman' and hence a 'warrior'.[9]

W. Robinson also suggested some related theories of the origin of the word 'Naga'. He writes that "the origin of the word is unknown, but it has been supposed by some to have been derived from the Sanskrit word 'Nagna' and applied in derision to the people, from the paucity of their clothing, but there seems a little foundation for this etymological derivation as the term has never been known to be applied by the Bengalese to either to the Khasis or the Garos with whom they were far better aquainted than with the Nagas; and besides, the Garos are habitually accustomed to a greater degree of nudity than any of the Naga tribes with whom we are acquainted with."[10]

The collective designation of the origin of the word 'Naga', writes E.A. Gait, by which the Nagas are known to the Assamese seems to be derived as suggested by Holcombe and Peal from 'Nok' which means 'folk' in some of the tribal dialects (Nok or Noka means people). He suggested that there was some connection between this and the Sanskrit 'Noka'.[11] The Burmese also called 'Naka' which means people with pierced ears. " The word 'Naga' is said to be another form of 'Naka' as the Nagas both man and woman pierced their ears."[12]

Verrier Elwin suggests that the probability of the origin of the word Naga from the word 'Nok' or people which is its meaning in a few Tibeto-Burman languages as in Garo, Nocte and Ao.[13]

Then the origin of the word Naga is still a mystery? It is highly possible that the word Naga is given by the Assamese, Bengalis and Burmese. It can also be assumed that the term Naga is generally defined as a political construct and as a cultural abstraction.

B. Linguistic and Anthropological Account of the Nagas

Nagas comprise the various tribes of Mongoloid race with distinct culture, laws and customs. Various theories of origin of the Nagas are also linked with the head-hunters of Malay and the races of the southern seas on the one hand and traced back to China on the other.[14] Whatever history available today is based on the oral tradition and folklore and songs.

According to some linguists and anthropologists, the Nagas belong to Tibeto-Burman family and sub families of the Tibeto Chinese race. Comparative philology agreed to point out that "the Nagas were among those who came down through Tibet to the Brahmaputra valley and the valleys of the Chindwin, Irrawady, Salwin, Mekong, etc, but were forced out of there by successive Tibeto-Chinese invaders and driven into the mountains where they eventually settled down.[15] There can be little doubt that before the Nagas came to the present areas they must have wandered for some years. The Burma census report also indicates migration of Nagas from region in western China between the source of the Yangste Kiang and Huwang-Ho river."[16]

The different philologists linguistically classified the race of the Nagas. The classification of Sir George A. Grierson is now generally accepted (vide census of India 1911). According to this classification, "Naga is of the Tibeto-Chinese family, Tibeto Burman sub family, Assam Burmese branch, group Naga sub group Western Naga."[17]

None of the tribes is of pure blood. Many races are found among the Nagas like Negrito race, later on Austric race of Kol-Annau or Mon Khmer types. Grouped as Indo-Mongoloid, but the Caucasis element is present among the Nagas in a remarkable degree, as a result, the Mongoloid facial and features are softened down in the Naga tribes.[18]

Most of the Naga tribes could be traced back to the Mon Khmer and Bodo races, the Thai races and a fourth races of southern origin akin to some of the inhabitants of the Philippines and Borneo and other parts of Indonesia. The legend of the Nagas have a similar culture with the natives of Borneo, a common traditional way of head-hunting, and with the Philippines and Formosa, the common system of terraced cultivation and also with the Indonesian as both use the loin-loom for weaving the embroidery which resembles in both the Naga and Indonesian clothes.[19] According to W.C. Smith, the Nagas and the Indonesians have a similar culture traits and physical characteristics. He traces out some of the Naga affinities to "the Dyaks and Kayaus of Borneo, the Battak of

Sumatra, certain groups of Formosa, the Igorot and Ifugas and several other groups in the Phillipines."[20]

Again W.C. Smith in his *'Ao Naga Tribe of Assam'* (London, 1925) has given 13 outstanding characteristics which are common to the Nagas even though they speak different languages, which "he attaches racially to the Indonesians, that is the people of Malaya and the islands of Indonesia. These are (i) head-hunting, (ii) Common sleeping house for the unmarried men, which are taboo to women, (iii) dwelling house built on post and piles, (iv) disposal of the dead on raised platform, (v) a sort of trial marriage or great freedom of intercourse between the sexes before marriage, (vi) betel-chewing (vii) aversion to milk as an article of diet, (viii) tatooing by pricking, (ix) absence of any powerful political organisation, (x) the double cylinder vertical forge, (xi) the simple loom for weaving cloth, (xii) a large quadriangular or hexagonal shield, and (xiii) residence in hilly regions with a crude form of agriculture."[21] There are also many closely parallel culture of the Nagas with those hilly tracts of Formosa, Indonesia and of Oceania.

The Nagas have also complex linguistic diversity. There is no common language among the Naga tribes. Each tribe has one or more dialects, which are unintelligible except through the medium of a third dialect by which they converse together. The lack of common language is mainly due to the composition of different stocks, languages and stages of migration from various routes and directions.

The area now occupied by the Naga tribes is known to have been subjected to atleast three immigrations of races from different directions. The first wave of migrants were the Maos, Angamis, Semas, Rengmas, Rongmei and Lothas, who moved from the south through the mountain fringes touching the valley of Manipur to the north, reached Mao area and settled in Kekruma, then moved north-eastward to Kezakenoma and Ura Academy, Kohima, where they spread and went into the different areas. Some groups went to the north west, some to the north-ward and some went to the west-ward,[22] which is now occupied presently by those tribes.

The second wave of immigrants comprised the Aos, Changs, Khiamnungans, Sangtams, Yimchunger and

Tangkhuls. This group is believed to have migrated from Thangdut, near Chindwin river in Burma by a different route, to their present hills.

The third group of immigrants is the Konyak Nagas who came to their present hills from the north-east of Burma and trace their orginal migration to Burma. Thus all of the Naga tribes came to settle in their respective present hills[23] in different waves of migration at different stages of time.

Though they came from different routes and directions before they migrated to the present hills, the Nagas must have settled somewhere together. They have something common in their origin, which is related with the caves and stone. Most of the Naga tribes indicate Meikhel* or its surrounding area as their place of origin. Some of the Naga tribes like Angamis, Aos, Semas, Lothas and Tangkhuls believe that their ancestors emerged from the caves and stone. But the origin of the Nagas is still obscure. One can only hope that perhaps, anthropologist and historians will be able to solve the long waited problem of the origins of the Nagas.

C. The Naga Relations with their Neighbours

i) Relations with the Ahoms

The Nagas were known to the outside world by the end of the 12th century A.D. It is a fact that there was occasional war and peace between the Nagas and their neighbours of Assam and Manipur. The first Naga arm encounter was with the Sukapha, the founder of Ahom kingdom in Assam. The Ahoms who belong to a Tai-race left Maulong in 1215 A.D. from Burma, with 900 men, women and children, with eight nobles, two elephants and 300 horses led by Prince Sukapha and entered into north-east of Assam. On the way to Brahmaputra valley they came through the Patkai range.[24] On eastern Naga Hills, they wandered for about 13 years making occasional raids on villages.[25] When they reached the boundary of Eastern Naga country of Nocte, Wancho and Tangsa in 1228

* Mekhel is a place in Mao area of Manipur believed to be the place of origin from where the Nagas spread to different directions.

A.D. they met stiff resistance from the eastern Nagas who challenged them for trespassing into their territory. But the Nagas were not able to prevent the mighty Ahoms.

However this strong resistance by the Nagas enraged the Prince Sukapha who defeated the Nagas and destroyed their villages, and killed a number of men, women and children. He treated the Nagas with 'ghastly barbarity' by forcefully feeding his captive to their relatives.[26] This barbarous treatment given by the Ahoms silenced the Nagas for quite some time and since then the hostility towards outsiders became deeply rooted in the minds of the Nagas and against encroachers of their land. They began to retaliate and used to raid the Ahoms frequently. This rivalry with the Ahoms continued till the 16th century.

Later on in the early part of 17th century the Ahom-Naga relationship improved during the reign of Sachimpha (1644–1648) and Jayadraj Sinha (1648–1663). That was the early part of the Ahom-Naga history of relationship. There were exchanges of gifts beween them such as gongs, spears, and daos by the Nagas and ear-rings, beads and cotton from the Ahoms. Some aspects of the Ahom-Naga relations were based on economy. The Ahoms policy towards the Nagas was based on a desire to control the 'brine springs' in eastern Naga territory which was manufacturing salt.[27] Before the British invasion of Assam, the salt was one of the rarest commodities for both the Ahoms and the Nagas. So the Ahoms maintained cordial relations with the Nagas to draw out sufficient quantities of salt from those brine wells. At the same time they exchange their products of rice, other food stuff and medicines.

Another aspect of Ahom policy was to stop the Nagas to carry out any raids in future. The Ahoms granted free revenue of lands and fishing water to the Nagas. These lands were called 'Naga Khats' in Assamese.[28] Subsequently, these 'Naga-Khats' became trading centres. Some of the Naga tribes like the Aos and the Lotha Nagas enjoyed such privileges. According to the history of Ahom-Naga relations this trading centres of Naga-Khats were opened by the king Godadhar Singh (1681–96). However king Godadhar Singh was once overthrown by king Laluk Buraphukan, and he took shelter in Naga hills for some years. After recapturing his kingdom, he was married to an Ao Naga girl called Sentishila. This folk tale of inter marriage remains fresh and clear in the minds of the Ao Nagas. In order to flourish trade and commerce between the Nagas and the Ahoms, king Laluk Buraphukan opened again the link road from Nokpu village to Rongpur calling it 'Assiranga Duar' after the name of Sentishila's father.[29] During the short reign of king Godadhar Singh, the Ahom-Naga relationship was peaceful and tranquil, but it was confined to the Nagas living in the low hills of plain areas bordering Assam.

The Ahom kings did not regard the Naga hills as their subjects,[30] and they never attempted to conquer the hills. Accordingly the relationship was only through a confederation and there was never any treaty and agreements signed by the two parties. The Nagas paid nominal tributes to Ahoms in the form of mithuns and other commodities but did not allow to extend their jurisdiction over any Naga hills.[31] The Ahom kings made no war with the Nagas to protect their frontier from the Burmese invasions, and when the Ahom kingdom was threatened from the Burmese military expansion, some of the Nagas were recruited by the Ahoms for their superior muscle strength, to build up a strong military army.

It is also said that during the Burmese invasion of Assam, thousands of Ahoms fled and were sheltered in Naga Hills till the Singphos of Burma had withdrawn from Assam. During this period, the Nagas had given assistance and support to Ahoms who later on recovered their kingdom.

The Ahom-Naga relationship lasted till the British took over Assam in the early part of 19th century. They developed a new attitude towards each other and became good neighbours for over 600 years.

According to J. Buttler, "the Naga territory was never considered an integral part of sovereignty of Assam."[32] Again another British writer Sir. Edward Gait, who wrote the History of Assam clarified that "the hilly tract inhabited by the various tribes known to us collectively as Nagas has never been subjugated by the Ahoms, and it was no part of the British policy to absorb it."[33]

ii) Relations with Manipuri and Kukis

Nagas relation with the Manipuris and the Kukis are quite different altogether. Only those Nagas who are living in the neighbourhood of the Manipur kingdom had exchanges and at times war. The Manipur Kings tried to extract tributes from Naga tribes of Angami, Mao and Tangkhul. Although racially, the Nagas, Manipuris and Kukis are allied Mongoloid stocks, the Nagas relation with them can be described as having wars as well as fraternal relationship.

In the beginning the Naga relations with the Manipuris were of friendship, mutual and cordial treatment to each other, inter-marriages, mutual exchange of visits and gifts,[34] but at times there were occassional wars between them. The nature of Naga-Manipuris relations was sometime confined to the collection of tributes from the Naga villages. During the head hunting period when there was war among the Nagas, the kings of Manipur assisted with arms to the friendly Nagas villages[35] against the other. At times, there were also occasional raids by the Angamis and Mao Nagas, whenever the Kings of Manipur tried to extend and impose duties against them. The subsequent invasions by the Nagas also caused great fear to the Manipuri kings. On the other hand, Manipur faced successive invasions by the Burmese from 1750 onwards.[36] To secure protection from the Burmese invasions, the kings of Manipur often sought help from the Nagas, Kukis and Assamese for alliances to challenge the Burmese. Intermittent war and peace existed between the Nagas and Manipuris, but the Nagas were not the subjects of the kings of Manipur.

The Nagas and the Kukis had unusual relations from olden days. Kukis are believed to be the last migrants from the Chin hills of Myanmar who came and occupied the foot hills of Manipur, encroached the Naga hills and ruled by the hereditary despotic chiefs.[37] It is argued by some that from the beginning the Tangkhul Nagas, Zemei, Liangmei and Rongmei (Zeliangrong) Nagas were the victims of the Kukis which they used to raid and punish them heavily. After the British invasion of Assam and Manipur in 1824, the British made the Kukis as frontliners in the war against Nagas. This further antagonised their relationship. Thus the Nagas and Kukis did not have any significant relationship. The relationship between the Nagas and Kukis can be said that the past history has a bearing on the contemporary pattern of Kukis-Naga relationship.

REFERENCES

1. J.P. Mills, *"The Lotha Nagas"*, Oxford University Press, Bombay, (Reprinted by Government of Nagaland), 1973, P. XV.
2. NSF Seminar Paper., *"The Naga Problem: An Account"*. New Delhi, 1985, p. 2.
3. J.P. Mills, n. 1, P. XVII.
4. C.V. Furer-. Haimendorf, *"The Naked Nagas"*, London, 1939, p. 1.
5. Alemchiba, *"A Brief Historical Account of Nagaland"*, The Naga Institute of Culture, Kohima, Nagaland, 1970, p. 26.
6. Ibid., p. 26, Quoted from Geographia. VII, ii, p. 18, p. 22.
7. Horam, *"Naga Polity"*, Reprinted, Low Price Publications Delhi, 1992, p. 22.
8. J.H. Hutton, *"Angami Nagas"* Oxford University Press, London, 1969, (Reprinted by Government of Nagaland), 1969, p. 5.
9. Asoso Yonuo, *"The Rising Nagas"*, Vivek Publishing House, New Delhi, 1979, p. 42.
10. Alemchiba, n. 5, p. 4, Quoted from the Eluri 'India, N.E.F. in the 19th century (1962), pp. 26–28.
11. Alemchiba, n. 5, p. 22.
12. Horam, n. 5, p. 25.
13. Verrier Elwin, *"Nagaland"* (Shillong, 1961), p. 4, quoted by Alemchiba, ibid., p. 23.
14. Hutton, n. 8, p. 8.
15. George, A. Grierson, *"Linguistic Survey of India"*, vol. 1 . part 1, Tibeto Burman Family, Calcutta, 1847, p. 42, quoted in NSF Seminar Paper, 1995, p. 1.
16. *Burma Census Report of 1911*, p. 225, quoted n. 5, p. 18.
17. Hutton, n. 8, p. 8.
18. Horam, n. 7, pp. 28–29.
19. Ibid., n. 7, p. 29.
20. Alemchiba, "The Ao Naga Tribes of Assam" (1925) quoted from 'The Ao Naga Tribes of Assam', W.C. Smith, in n. 5, p. 12.
21. Ibid., n. 5, p. 4.
22. Alemchiba, n. 5, p. 20.
23. Asoso, n. 9, p. 39.
24. Alemchiba, n. 5, p. 30.
25. Ibid, n. 5, p. 31.
26. Horam, n. 7, p. 25.
27. Mackenzie, *"The North-East Frontier of India"*, Mittal Publications, New Delhi, 1979, p. 91.

28. Asoso, n. 9, p. 56.
29. Bendangangshi *"Glimpses of Naga History"*, Published by Naga Patriots from Soyim, Mokukchung, Nagaland, (1993), p. 11.
30. Alemchiba, n. 5, p. 39.
31. Ibid., n. 5, p. 40.
32. Quoted by Alemchiba, n. 5, p. 40, from A Sketch of Assam (1847), p. 152.
33. Gait, E., "History of Assam", Thacker Spink & Co. Ltd., Calcutta, 1933. p. 366.
34. Asoso, n. 9, p. 46.
35. Ibid., n. 9, p. 50.
36. Ibid., n. 9, p. 50.
37. Ibid., n. 9, p. 52.

CHAPTER TWO

British Occupation of Naga Hills: (1832–1879)

The beginning of the 19th century marked the struggle for supremacy between the British and Burmese over Assam and north-east frontier which ended up with the First Anglo-Burmese War on 24th February 1824. In this war the Britishers defeated the Burmese and drove them out from Assam, and by the treaty of Yandaboo in 1826, Assam was brought under British control. The conflict occured due to the attempt of the later to have a hold over Assam and to exploit the vast economic potential of the Brahmaputra valley.[1] Historically no foreign country had conquered the Nagas. It was only by the end of the 19th century, the British came and colonised some parts of the Naga hills. This is now called the southern part of Nagaland.

From the beginning the Nagas have not shown much interest for unity. Inter tribal feud was very much prevalent among the Nagas, and head hunting was a sort of trophy collection. In that kind of situation the British entered through the Naga hills on their way to Assam. The first ever Britishers to visit Naga hills was Captain Jenkins and Captain Pamberton in January 1832 with 700 soldiers and 800 coolies. With the help of King Gambheer Singh of Manipur, they marched from Manipur to Assam through the Angami Naga Hills. The party suffered heavily at the hands of the warlike tribes of the Nagas, who attacked them repeatedly in every step of the roads.[2] They faced a lot of hardships because of stiff resistance from the Angami Nagas.

The British occupation of Assam marked the beginning of punitive expeditions against the Naga hills from 1839 onwards to safeguard the plain areas of Assam from the warlike Nagas. Mr. Grange, Sub Assistant at Nowgong conducted the first expedition to investigate the causes of the Naga raids, and "endeavour to punish the Chiefs of the large villages of Khonoma and Mezoma,"[3] but the expedition returned without achieving much success due to the "unflinching Naga resistance and partly because of mismanagement by the British authorities."[4]

However Mr. Grange's second expedition of 1840, succeeded to some extend in which he burnt down five villages and captured eleven Naga prisoners,[5] then reached an agreement with the hostile Nagas to pay tributes to the British. But in 1844, instead of paying tributes to the British the Nagas indulged and committed a series of raids on the neighbouring plain areas. Hence forth, the British government put forward policy for retaliation and adopted defensive military actions against the Nagas. During 1849–50 as many as 10 expeditions were sent under the command of Lieutenant Vincent. In his tenth expedition, he captured a strong Naga fort at Khonoma and fought a bloody battle against the masses of the tribes of Kekrema. But the British troops were withdrawn in March 1851 from the hills.[6] This was the turning point of the British policy towards the Nagas. Consequently, Lord Dalhousie the then Governor General of India laid down a policy of non interference in Naga hills, "our possessions could bring no profit to us, and would be as costly to us it would be unproductive"... "but to occupy the country was in their instance better than to let it alone"[7] to protect the administrative areas.

Despite all the policies formulated by the British governors, Nagas frequently raided the plainsmen. According to the sources from 1854 to 1865 the Angami Nagas committed 19 raids, in which 232 people including some British officers were killed.

A. Establishment of Naga Hills District—1866

In order to check the war like Nagas from further outrages, the British government created the Naga Hills District in 1866 with its headquarters at Samaguting (Chumukedima) for administrative and political convenience. The creation of the District could also be seen as the Government's policy to check and protect the plain people from Naga's raids. However, this was the first step by the British who advocated the divide and rule policy to push the political boundary in Naga hills. Although "the permanent establishment of a British officer in the Angami Naga country had the effect of stopping the annual raids upon the British territory at the time of Gregory,"[8] who was appointed as the first Deputy Commissioner of the Naga Hills. In march 1871 when Captain Butler took in charge of the Deputy Commissioner from Gregory in the Naga Hills, the Nagas committed raids in Manipur on the question of the demarcation of the boundary. To resolve the complications of the disputes he adopted a bolder policy in which extensive explorations were proposed, and the clear definition of boundary lines and local limits was postulated as essential to any proper working of the scheme. This view was eventually accepted by the supreme British government.[9]

i) Inner Line Regulation, 1873

During the period of 1869–73, the major subject taken up by the British was for expansion of tea plantation in the Naga Hills of Assam. The rapid expansion of tea plantation in the frontiers of Naga hills aroused great resentment against the British and caused lot of disturbances to the tea planters. In order to control the problem "by 1873 under the Chin Hills Regulation and the Bengal Eastern Frontier Regulation, the Inner Line Regulation was enforced prohibiting British India subjects from entering the Naga Hills without prior permission."[10]

> Thus, "The Inner Line Regulation was the first law promulgated in Assam under the authority conferred by the Statute 33 Vict. ..., Chapter 3, which had given the Government of India power of summary legislation for backward tracts. Such laws are made to distinguish them from the Acts or Laws passed after discussion in the legislature."[11]

This Regulation drew certain line on the ground without necessary permission and was operated for the protection of both the Nagas and the plainsmen. And again it was implied to the tea planters to pay compensation to the Nagas for the land occupied by tea estates which were lying beyond the Inner Line.[12]

Meanwhile Major Godwin-Austin was deputed to Naga hills in 1874 to explore the eastern boundary from Talizo Peak eastward to the watershed between the confluence of the Brahmaputra and Irrawady unto the Patkai Pass for the purpose of laying down the boundary line between Manipur and the Naga hills and not as between Manipur and British territory.[13] The result of his expedition was not altogether satisfactory, because of the thick forest, terrain and hostility by the Nagas.

Then the Naga hills were made under the charge of the Chief Commissioner of Assam in February, 1874.[14] From 1874–1878, the British Government conducted many surveys and operations, but had brought the loss of many officers, and coolies at the hands of the Nagas including Captian Butler, the Deputy Commissioner in 1875, who was a qualified and influential over the Naga tribes and most able and enthusiastic officer killed in ambush at the village of Pangti (Lotha Naga Village). For a more effective operation in the Naga hills the British Headquarters were shifted to Wokha (Lotha area) in 1875, from Samaguating. The purpose of shifting the headquarters was to influence the neighbouring tribes, and to protect the inroads of the Nagas on the borders for their convenience.

Later on the permanent site for the future political officers' headquarters was shifted in March 1878, from Wokha to Kohima, the principal Angami village and the Manipur frontier line. Till 1947, Kohima was the headquarters of the British India Government.

ii) Occupation of Kohima, 1879–1880

The occupation of Kohima by the British was the turning point of the last war of Naga independence against the imperialist. In July 1878, the government of British India communicated to the new Chief Commissioner Sir. S.C. Bayley, its general view of the more forward policy advocated by Colonel Keating to bring the Nagas into complete submission.[15] Such designs propagated by the British had forced the Nagas to defend their country. Amidst all these, there was an inter tribal feud among the Angami Nagas. To prevent and to punish the guilty villages by fine and penalties, Damant, the political officer of Naga hills in the early part of 1879–80, put the British policy into action. At the same time, some complications occurred in April 1879, when a policeman was shot dead by a Naga to obtain the rifle while he was escorting the mail runner who seized the rifle. This report came to the office of Damant, but the killer was left untracked. In May Damant came to know that Khonoma village was acquiring arms and ammunitions, and "in the attitude of Khonoma was decidedly threatening that Damant proposed to organise a hostile expedition against it after the monsoon; but even at this time Khonoma was apparently divided against itself."[16] He was full of confidence with no fear and suspicion from the Nagas, but at that time the Angami Nagas were preparing for the war against the British and drive them out from the Naga soil.

> On 13th of October, 1879 Mr. Damant set out on his expedition accompanied by an escort of 21 military and 65 police"[17] to three Angami villages, Jotsoma, Khonoma, and Mezoma. Before he started to Jotsoma "an ominous sign was on its way"[18] as warned by a Jotsoma interpreter who was very kind to Damant. The interpreter advised him not to proceed to Khonoma as the people were preparing war against Britishers. Damant however replied that there was no danger for him, and went straight to the village. As soon as he entered the fortress gate of Khonoma village an enraged military of the village shot him on the spot. This was followed by a volley of bullets on his escorts suffering a loss of 25 soldiers, three domestic servants and 19 wounded.[19]

The news of this disaster encounter immediately spread like wild fire and reached the British Headquarters in Kohima the same afternoon. The Military and civil incharge of the garrison entrusted Mr. Cawley, District Superintendent of Police at Kohima to make preparation for sudden attack with a force of 180 Police.[20] A message was sent to Mr. Hinde, the Extra Assistant Commissioner in charge of Wokha, 57 miles away from Kohima and Colonel Johnstone at Imphal. Then Hinde reached the Kohima on 19th October with a heavy war preparation of 40 sepoys and 22 policemen. Equally a great war game was prepared by the warrior Angami Nagas to defend their motherland. The other thirteen Angami villages[21] also joined Khonoma in the uprising, they blocked Kohima for eleven days, until the relief reached from Manipur.[22]

After receiving the news of the murder of Damant, Colonel Johnstone, the Political Agent of Manipur, asked the King of Manipur to put a force of 2,000 Manipuri troops at his disposal for the vengeance against the Angami Nagas. The force under the command of a minister and the King's two sons started the next day and covered a distance of nearly hundred miles, over a roadless hills in the jungle and most difficult terrains and reach Kohima in five days.[23] On the following day the British attacked Khonoma. However it was not an easy task for the British force to capture the stronghold of Khonoma. Even by using modern weapons the war lasted for a whole day. But at nightfall, they captured the lower portion of Khonoma village. This war has been considered as one of the severest war ever known in the Naga hills. Finally the superior arms defeated the inferior. And the warrior Nagas evacuated the remaining upper portion of the village and fled to the jungles in the night itself. The following day the British force occupied the village and destroyed the site of opposition. Even Jotsoma, lying close by Khonoma was captured on 27th November and a portion of the village was burnt.[24] "The Nagas retreated to a strongly fortified position on a crest of the Burrail range, where, as their access to their fields and houses was completely cut off" In the war the Britishers lost two officers and subedar Major of the 44th S.L.I. was killed, two British and two native officers were heavily wounded and 44 of the rank and file were killed and badly wounded.[25]

In consequent to the war, the Angami Nagas were punished heavily, fined in grain, cash and unpaid labour were levied upon them by the British. Nagas lost the war but the victory of British imperialist could not win over the Naga's sentiment. The hostile spirit, resistance against the outsiders and freedom for their country still remained the same. The war of Khonoma was one of the remarkable events of the Nagas uprising among the Naga history.

Consequent to the fall of Khonoma village in 1879, the other Naga villages also submitted to the British, and by 1881, the British imperialist had succeeded in establishing their authority over the then Naga Hills District.

B. British Policy from 1881 to 1947

i) Administrative Policy

The occupation of Naga Hills by the British was initially to protect the plainsmen from Naga raids. But later on mainly after the occupation of Kohima following the battle of Khonoma 1879, they started to penetrate the neighbouring Naga hills for their administrative as well as political convenience. Sir Robert Reid writes "The first decision to make the Naga Hills a British district was taken in 1881.... The necessity of protecting the borders of Nowgong, Sibsagar against raiding Nagas which in the early days compelled us to penetrate into the hills little by little ceased with the formation of the Naga Hill District. But the process of penetration went inexorably, if irregularly. It was impossible to draw a line as the boundary of our areas of control and to say that we should be blind and deaf to all that went on across that line. The trans frontier Nagas raid on our administered village are involved in dispute with the former head hunting and massacres go on just across the border and under the very noses of our officers. In such conditions local officers inevitably, and with reason, clamour for forward policy. The Chief Commissioner sometimes supports them, sometimes he does not. The Government of British India is nearly always reluctant. But the frontier moves forward."[26] From 1881 onwards they continued their punitive expeditions and annexed more territory of the Naga hill which was brought under their control till

1947, with the exception of Tuensang Areas (hills) which remained unconquered and almost unvisited by the British.

Mr. McCabe, the then Deputy Commissioner of Naga Hills 1881–94 put to work an annexation policy which was carried out in a gradual way and "based on four general principles: (a) to insist a strict obedience within his own jurisdiction; (b) to punish villages within his jurisdiction for all raids committed against trans-frontier villages; (c) to punish trans-frontier villages for raids against this-frontier villages; (d) as far as possible to mediate in disputes between villages adjacent to the frontier."[27]

The inter tribal war and head hunting among the Nagas in the trans frontier areas was very rampant causing much inconvenience to the British administered areas. More expeditions were therefore designed to protect their administrative territory.

The annexation policy adopted by Mr. McCabe brought more Naga hills under their control, and at the same time the tribal feud and head hunting among the Nagas were also reduced. One positive thing about the British administrative policy in the Naga hills was their non-interference in the Naga culture and custom, tradition and indigenous village administration. These were completely looked after by the village headmen (Gaonburas) who decided any dispute both of civil and criminal nature according to customary laws.

The occupation of the Ao country in 1888 was followed by the establishment of a sub division at Mokokchung. For their administrative convenience, the Naga Hills district was divided into sub-divisions of Kohima and Mokokchung under a Deputy Commissioner. The Deputy Commissioner who looked after the British Hill District resolved "the inter tribal quarrel to those cases where they involved: (1) outrages on British subjects, (2) violation of Inner Line (3) danger to the interest of people dwelling inside the British borders by reasons of the proximity of disturbance outside, such disturbances for instance, as would be likely to be intimidate to coolies employed upon tea estates or cultivators"[28] This order was passed on to the Deputy Commissioner of Naga Hills and Sibsagar by the Governor General of India. In order to implement the Government's instruction, "the Chief Commissioner then ordered the Deputy Commissioner of Naga Hills to make two more expeditions (a) to a number of eastern Angami villages along the Manipur border to the east of Kohima and outside the existing boundary of the Naga Hill district, and (b) to a number of Ao villages east of Wokha. Again the same instruction was ordered to the Deputy Commissioner of Sibsagar to visit the Konyak villages to the east of the boundary."[29] Any dispute arising beyond the trans border areas was a British subject to interfere and punish them.

Another policy adopted by the British government was to prevent carrying the daos and spears in the market and other public places. The Government considered that this prohibition would cut down the number of attacks by the Nagas. This imposition was in fact against the tradition of the Nagas for whom the carrying of daos and spears was a way of life besides for the protection against wild animals and enemies as well. This policy did not have much affect on the Nagas.

After the occupation of some parts of Naga Hills the British established two administrative units to extend their authority on the restive Nagas. They initiated imposing of annual House Taxes discriminately as Rs. 3 (three) on the Angamis and Rs. 2 (two) on the others with Rs. 5 (five) on the foreigners.[30] The Nagas were made to pay the House Tax as an acknowledgement of British suzerainty over them and failure of payment met punitive measures and reprisals.

However, some Nagas refused to pay the extraneous House Tax imposed by the British administration as it was too exorbitant. Thus, the Khonoma War, which was a result of the Naga defiant against the British might by refusing to pay the tax, occurred in 1879.

One important duty of the Deputy Commissioner of the Naga Hills was to tour the whole Naga Hills at least one third of the year, no matter how inaccessible the way might be, and find out the problems and disputes of the villages on the spot. The Deputy Commissioner was made the over all incharge of the district for an effective administrative convenience. The colonial government however failed to develop the Naga Hills and education of the people was totally neglected.

ii) Advent of the Christianity

Christianity came to the Naga Hills through the American Baptist Missionaries who came and preached the love of Christ to the head hunting Nagas. Before the advent of Christianity, the warlike Nagas were frequently indulging in raids and head hunting. Life was not secured as neighbours raid each other in search of heads for trophies. Religion being professed was a form of animism.

The American Baptist Missionaries came risking and sacrificing their lives to preach the Gospel of Christ and won the Nagas from head hunting.

The first American Missionary who came to the Naga hills was Rev. Mills Bronson. He arrived in 1839–40 at Namsang, a village in the Tirap frontier. But he did not accomplish much in the Naga hills as he had to leave the place due to illness, demise of his sister and other misfortunes.[31] In his short stay in the hills he established a Mission school to teach the three R's and Gospel of Christ to the Nagas. In the year 1869, Dr. E.W. Clark came to Sibsagar to join the Missionary work. His attention was attracted by the war like Nagas and his mind immediately turned to the Ao Naga tribe. In 1871, "he engaged an Assamese Christian named Godhula to acquire language from the Aos to stay there."[32] For entering the Naga hills, a special permission from the Deputy Commissioner was necessary as it was restricted to the white people. After obtaining the permission, Dr. E.W. Clark entered the Ao Naga hills of Dickahaimong (village of Molungkimong) and made preparations for his stay. This was the beginning of American Mission activities in the Naga hills.

Meanwhile, a few Ao Nagas were baptised in Sibsagar by the Missionaries. In this manner, Christianity slowly spread into the Naga Hills making the Nagas to give up the practise of their old religion and their conversion to the new religion. It was through the American Baptist Missionaries that the Nagas were weaned away from the practices of head hunting and the old religion and were converted into Christianity which taught them to be more loving and peaceful. The American Baptist Mission established 16 schools for the Nagas (and ushered in modern education to the Nagas).. In comparison, the British Missionaries succeeded in establishing only 6 (six) primary schools during the years 1881 to 1947.[33]

There are some writers who are of the opinion that the Naga ethnic movement was instigated by the American Missionaries. In 1953 the then Home Minister Dr. K.N. Katju, made a strong statement in the Parliament to the effect that Missionary activities should be restricted in Naga Hills, as their work in politics was not clear. Thus the Government of India issued an order for all the foreign missionary to leave Nagaland.[34] However it is not true to say that foreign missionaries instigated the Naga movement. Their contribution was confined to providing religion and modern education which made the Naga aware of his surroundings and his ethnic identity and political rights, and of the universal rights shared by all human beings.

iii) Impact of the First World War

The impact of the First World War was not felt much in the Naga Hills except for the sending of labour corps of 2,000 Nagas to France by the British. But this served as an opportunity for the Nagas to see the outside world and to develop a strong sense of their ethnic identity. This new awareness they gained also made them more assertive of their differences with the rest of the British Government.

As a consequence, after the First World War the Naga Club was formed in Kohima in the year 1918. This was formed on the advise and initiative of the British whose aim was to unite all the Naga tribes and to bring them into one platform. This was a "watershed" in the history of the Nagas in that it was the first organisation to have representatives of most of the Naga tribes, Government servants and leading headmen of villages. The aim of the club was both social and political in nature, and also an attempt to wean over the Nagas from their inter tribal feuds and foster solidarity amongst them. Later it was followed by the formation of the first Tribal Council in 1923 by the Lothas subsequently followed by Aos in 1928.

The Naga Hills District was declared as 'Backward Tract' in 1921. It was placed under British Assam Province under section 52 (2) of the Government of India Act, 1919, purely for their administrative convenience. This Act also introduced what was known as "Dyarchy System" by which state subjects were divided into Reserved and Transferred subjects. In 1925, under the Transferred subject, forest lands were transferred to the districts of Sibsagar and Nowgong. Unfortunately now, the state of Assam makes claims that it has inherited the transferred forest lands from the British imperialists and has so far refused to return them to the Nagas.[35]

iv) Simon Commission

The British India was passing through political turmoil and rebellions in the early 1920s. The Indian National Congress was launching a non violent movement under the charismatic leadership of Mahatma Gandhi for India's independence from the British yoke. Seeing the situation of British India, the British Home Government set up a statutory commission under the Chairmanship of Sir John Simon known as the *Simon Commission* in 1928 to study the British India situation for future policy. When the visit of the Simon Commission was imminent, the Nagas expressed their desire for independence to Sir. J.H. Hutton who had served 'the distinction of about twenty years of Deputy Commissioner in Naga Hills'[36] who convened a meeting to ascertain their wishes after the British left India. J.H. Hutton's documents say, *"It is the purpose of this note to show that the interest of hill districts will not only served by having them included proposed the reforms but they will suffer very serious detriment by being tied up to the politically more advanced plains district while latter will suffer in the future by being joined with people of an irreconcilable culture in an unnatural union which can ultimately only entail discomfort for both parties."*[37] This report of J.H. Hutton brought the Simon Commission to Kohima on 10th January 1929. The Naga Club, representing the Naga People submitted a memorandum to the Commission demanding "that we should not be put at the mercy of the people, who could never have conquered us, and to whom we were never subjected, but to leave us alone, to determine for ourselves (our future as) in ancient times."[38] That was the first Naga political document ever submitted to a foreign ruler. The report of the Simon Commission to replace the phrase 'Backward Tract' of the Government of India Act, 1919, was debated in the House of Common in 1935. The British recognised the Naga claim to be treated separately from the British India Act 1935 renamed the Naga Hills District the 'Naga Hills Excluded Area'. It was henceforth directly administered by the Governor of Assam (The House of Commons Session 1934–35, Bill 17(1) pp. 56–57). In the words of Colonel Wedgewood " they (Nagas) must not be converted from good Nagas or whatever they are into bad Hindus, for no prominent India politicians have ever displayed the slightest interest in this subject as compared with Europeans who had a natural and strong sympathy with these people"[39]

Sir Robert Reid, the then Governor of Assam explained the implication of excluded and partially excluded areas thus, "Constitutionally only the two valley of Assam came within the ambit of the Reform Act of 1935 and so fell under full control by the Cabinet of elected members. The Hill districts meaning the Balipara Frontier Tract, Sadya Frontier Tract, Naga Hills and Lushai Hills were 'excluded'. They were administered by the Governor 'in his discretion'. But the partially 'excluded areas' comprising the Khasi and Jaintia, the Garo and Mekir Hills, enjoyed the privileges to elect members to the Legislature and Ministry was primarily responsible for the administration. But by Section 52(a) of the Act the Governor was charged with special responsibility for their 'Peace and Good Government' a responsibility which was obvious from the start would be and indeed was, very hard to discharge."[40] The use of the words 'Excluded' and partially 'Excluded' have been thoroughly exploited politically and wrongly interpreted.

v) Zeliangrong Movement: 1931–1941

In the late 1920s Zeliangrong movement was launched by Jadonang and later on by Gaidinliu in the north west hills of Manipur. Jadonang, who initiated this uprising was a Kabui Naga. His aim was to unite three constituents of Naga tribes: the Zemeis, Liangmeis and Rongmeis (Zeliangrong) to drive away the British as well as Kukis who were regarded as outsiders.[41] Jadonang was supposed to have the powers of a 'sorcerer' and the kacha Nagas "believing that he is the 'Messiah' for whom they have been waiting for sent him large number of mithuns and domesticated gayals as tributes."[42] The objective of the uprising was a "socio religious reformation and political goal to separate the Zeliangrong from the British regime. And his aim was to establish Naga Raj."[43] But before achieving his goal, he was implicated and sentenced to death on 13th June 1931.[44] After his execution, Gaidinliu, a young unmarried girl of only 17 years old carried the movement by organising armed rebellion which was also suppressed in 1932.[45] Jadonang and Gaidinliu called on the people to disobey the oppressive laws of the British regime and not to pay house tax. Jadonang's religious ideas were 'crystallised' in the 'Heraka cult' by Gaidinliu who was regarded as his 'spiritual successor.'[46] Gaidinliu was 'wanted' on the charge of murder and arrested in September 1932. The 'Heraka Cult' which was revived by Gaidinliu spread over a large area of the Naga hills, Manipur and the North Cachar Hills. Her capture saved a situation of grave danger of a serious outbreak.[47] But finally she was sentenced to life imprisonment. She was released after 1947 by the Government of India, which acknowledged her as a patriotic freedom fighter. The late Prime Minister Jawaharlal Nehru referred to her as Rani. Since then she came to be known as Rani Gaidinliu, and "she was recognised as a political sufferer, awarded pension.[48] But it has been argued that she did not fought for the Indian freedom struggle. Moreover none of the Nagas participated in the Indian National Congress which led to the Indian freedom struggle. Gaidinliu in fact fought for the unification of Zeliangrong, freedom from foreign rule, reform the practice of 'Hereka Cult and to establish the Naga Raj'.

vi) Nagas in the Second World War

The outbreak of the Second World War was of great significance in the History of the Nagas. When the Japanese occupied Burma, their imminent invasion of Manipur and the Naga hills gave a serious threat to the Allied forces. The seizing of Kohima (capital of Nagaland) was equally important for both the Japanese and the Allied power. For the Japanese, it was necessary to make their conquest of South-East Asia, while for the Allied power the defence of Kohima was very vital to defend the whole of India sub continent.[49] "In September 1943, General Kawabe, the Japanese Commander-in-Chief in Burma and Subhas Chandra Bose, the Supreme Commander of the Indian National Army decided to launch an attack in the Chin Hills, Manipur and the Naga Hills.[50] A.Z. Phizo, an Angami Naga who went to Burma in 1933 also joined in the Indian National Army led by Subhas Chandra Bose as a corporal till 1944."[51] The main purpose of Subhas Chandra Bose and the Phizo 'game plan' was to bring the Japanese into the Naga Hills to defeat the British forces and to conquer the Indian sub continent for the freedom of India and the Nagas. INA led Subhas Chandra Bose was fighting for India independence from the British yoke and the Naga A.Z. Phizo joining with the INA was for the cause of the Nagas. The dream of Phizo unfortunately was not fulfilled. It was a great tragedy for the Nagas.

The Battle of Kohima was one of the fierest in the sub-continent. It is said to be the 'Waterloo' for the Japanese. When the Japanese fought the war in Kohima, the Nagas joined the Allied forces as coolies, guides, and supplied them with food stuff. The Nagas could capture a number of armies. This was made possible due to the loyalty and co-operation by the Nagas to the Allied forces. The combined forces defeated the Japanese in the battle of Kohima.

vii) The Significance of the Allied Forces Victory

The epitaph: *"When you go home tell them of us, and say for your tomorrow we gave our today"* in the heart of Kohima war Cemetery, symbolises the sacrifices and significance of the battle of Kohima.

In the aftermath of the Japanese defeat in the Battle of Kohima the Allied forces re-occupied Burma. A.Z. Phizo was arrested and imprisoned in the Central jail in Rangoon for seven months for the collaboration of Indian National Army. Phizo returned to Naga Hills in 1946 and joined in the Naga National Council (NNC).

viii) The Crown Colony Scheme

When the World War II broke out Indian subcontinent was passing through a period of chaos and turbulence. The subcontinent under the reign of the British joined hands with the Allied Forces against the Japanese, Italian and German Axis. At the same time India was struggling for its independence. By then the British colonialists realised that the subcontinent was about to end.[52]

Sir. Robert Reid who was the Governor of Assam from 1937–1942 realised the ethnic and cultural differences between the Naga tribes and the rest of British India and Burma reccommended a scheme to carve out a 'Trust Territory' "comprising of Naga hills areas of Assam and the upper part of Burma inhabited by tribal people to form a Crown Colony."[53]

This proposal was mooted by Sir Robert Reid to form a new state which would be controlled not from Delhi but from the White Hall. In his confidential report Sir Robert Ried proposed that:

> "We have no right to allow this great body of non-Indian animist and Christians to be drawn into the struggle between Hindus and Muslims which is now and will be in the future politics in India proper.... They cannot be left to Indian political leaders neither knowledge, interest nor feeling for the areas. In any case if my main premise of separation from India is accepted their intervention could scarcely arise .... Personally, I am in favour of Dr. Hutton's idea of a North-East Province vaguely embracing all the hill fringes from Lushai (or Lakher) land on the south right round to the Balipara Frontier tract on the north, embracing on the way Chittagong hill tracts of Bengal and the Nagas and Chins of Burma and perhaps the Shan state too. I could put this under a Chief Commissioner and he in turn could, I imagine, have to be divorced (as in Burma) from the control of the government of India (presumably a federal body by them) and put perhaps under some appropriate department of Whitehall."[54]

Robert Reid further notes:

> "Those of us who, before 1947, were speculating on the future of the hill were very anxious that they should not be made a plaything of Indian politics and when I retired in 1943, I tried to rouse the interest in this problem at home but everyone was rightly concentrating on winning to war, and any how, India's North-East Frontier was much too small to hope for any special treatment in the post war discussions. We had thought of setting up some sort of agency to embrace the whole north-east frontier fringe, and to exclude it from the general round of Indian politics with which it had no affinity. But the only way to ensure this would have been somehow to separate this area from the territory being handed over, and British India without qualifications was being transferred to the successor governments of India and Pakistan. So it would not work. The North-Eastern Frontier fringe might within the meaning of the Reform Act of 1935 be an excluded area, but it was still part of British India."[55] But the Crown Colony scheme could not be implemented.

After Sir Robert Reid, Sir Reginald Coupland, a constitutional expert, reviewed Sir Robert Ried proposal and introduced a new proposal famously known as "Coupland Plan". This plan emphasized that " the Government of India and Burma might have a treaty with the British and it should take share of responsibilities for the areas as 'Trust Territory'. In support of the Plan, he stated 'there is one major area which seems to call for a special treatment, the hill tracts on the north-east frontier of Assam and the adjoin similar hill tracts on the north west frontier of Burma. The inhabitants of both areas are alike in races and culture. They are not Indians or Burma Nation."[56] But the 'Coupland Plan' was ultimately put in cold storage due to a change of hands in the government. Sir Winston Churchill of the Conservative Party was put out of power, and the Labour Government which subsequently took over the power was not interested in any confrontation in the subcontinent. Despite that "the Nagas opposed it vehemently since they had no affection to any kind of British imperialism and colonialism."[57] But the Nagas could not anticipate the possible outcome and consequences. They presumed that when the British quit India they would get independence. But that did not happen. It was due to the myopic view of the Nagas who were reluctant to extend support for the British Plans. Lamenting the Naga stand Robert Ried wrote: "If the Nagas had lent slightest support or encouragement to this scheme, the colony might have been a reality."[58]

C. The Cultural and Societal Frames of Reference of the Nagas

In order to understand the salience and relevance of the Naga ethnic movement it is necessary to develop the cultural and societal frames of reference of the Naga cultural revolutionaries. Robert D. Crane's observation has explanatory significance: "The Naga who now have 3000 college graduates and are one of the most literate nations in Asia have began to conduct original research in their own obscure history. They are conscious of the fact that of all the peoples of Southeast Asia they alone have never once succumbed during the past two millennia to any of the waves of immigrants that periodically swept down into Southeast Asia from the north." Although the political obstacles are still daunting, the ideas and visions of the future held by Naga nationalists are based on the innate strength of traditional culture and therefore highly relevant to the structure of the decision making groups and the personality of individual Nagas. Naga culture is a living organism and affirms the existence of distinctive frame of mind. The Naga ethnic movement has combined the tribal values and organisation with a synergy of self-determination with the democratic principle. The Naga culture is tribally and socially constructed. Any effort to impose hegemonic atomisation and individualisation on the Nagas through political manipulation would come up against stronger demands.

D. Naga Decision-making Groups

Structure of Power Relation and Accepted Values of the International System

For conflict management to successfully eliminate the danger of ethnic instability ethnicity should be used for political purposes only if it is in harmony with the structure of power relations and the accepted values of the international system. If this is not the case the danger of "self determination" exhausting its legitimacy is always there. The Naga decision-making groups can generate bargaining leverage channelling ethnic conflicts away from violence provided there is some kind of equity of power and status so as to arrive at solutions which are appropriate. After British withdrawal from India it could have been agreed that there is no such thing as absolute sovereignty in international law and a real durable peace settlement could have been arrived at through institutional initiatives to build up a series of community councils and municipal arrangements. At the same time there would have been an increasing role for stable institutionalisation of Naga authority without all politics converging on the sovereign national state. It can be argued perhaps that by formulating its national security priorities and military-political interests without providing adequate measure of self-government to the Nagas, India created a focus on a hegemonic conception of Nagaland's connection with India. The later political struggle as a war of liberation may not have emerged if coercive assimilation had not been initially practiced.

REFERENCES

1. NSF Seminar Paper, n. 2, p. 3.
2. A.M. Mackenzie, n. 27, p. 101.
3. Ibid., n. 27, p. 104.
4. Horam, n. 7, p. 9.
5. Asoso, n. 9, p. 77.
6. Mackenzie, n. 27, p. 112.
7. Ibid, n. 27, pp. 113–115.
8. Ibid, n. 27, p. 122.

9. Ibid., n. 27, p. 124, quoted from the letter to Bengal, No. 1661, dated 24th July, 1873.
10. NSF Seminar Paper, n. 2, p. 4, quoted from Gait, n. 23, pp. 385–386.
11. Ibid., n. 33, pp. 386–387.
12. Asoso, n. 9, p. 94.
13. Asoso, n. 9, p. 95.
14. Mackenzie, n. 27, p. 124.
15. Mackenzie, n. 27, p. 133.
16. Ibid., n. 27, p. 134.
17. Mackenzie, n. 27, p. 135.
18. Asoso, n. 9, p. 101.
19. Mackenzie, n. 27, p. 35
20. Asoso, n. 9, p. 101.
21. Ibid., n. 9, p. 102.
22. Ibid, n. 9, p. 102.
23. Mackenzie, n. 2, p. 136.
24. Alemchiba, n. 5, pp. 90–91.
25. Mackenzie, n. 27, p. 137.
26. Sir Robert Reid, 'History of the Frontier Areas Bordering Assam from 1883–1941', Eastern Publication House, 1983, pp. 99–100.
27. Ibid., n. 63. p. 102, quoted from Assam Secretariat Judicial Department, file No. 149-J of 1884.
28. Ibid., n. 63, p. 104.
29. Ibid., n. 63, p. 104.
30. Asoso, n. 9, p. 110.
31. Ibid., n. 9, p. 114.
32. L. Wati, 'Facts and Growth of Naga Nationalism' mimeograph, (1993), p. 7.
33. Ibid., p. 8.
34. Ibid., p .8.
35. NSF Seminar Paper, n. 2, p. 4.
36. M. Rammuny, 'The World of Nagas', Northern Book Centre., New Delhi, 1988, p. 14.
37. Ibid., n. 73, p. 14, quoted from Simon Commission Report, Kohima Raj Bhavan Records.
38. Memorandum submitted to the Simon Commission by the Naga Club on 10th January, 1929.
39. NSF Seminar Paper, n. 2, p. 5.
40. Rammuny, n. 73, p. 16.
41. K.S. Singh, (Ed.), 'Tribal Movement in India', Vol. I., Manohar Publications, 1982., New Delhi, p. 54.
42. Robert Reid, n. 63, p. 167.
43. Singh, n. 78, p. 56.
44. Robert Reid, n. 63, p. 170.
45. Singh, n. 78, p. 56.
46. Robert Reid, n. 63, p. 170.
47. Ibid., p. 171.
48. Asoso, n. 9, p. 128, see Y.D. Gundevia, War and Peace in Nagaland, Palit and Palit Publishers, New Delhi 1975. p. 65. see also V.K. Anand, Conflict in Nagaland, Chanakya Publication, 1980. pp. 193–194.

49. Alemchiba, n. 5 p. 152.
50. Asoso, n. 9, p. 143
51. Ibid., n. 9, p. 199.
52. Ibid., n. 9, p. 139.
53. NSF Seminar Paper, n. 2, p. 5.
54. Ibid., n. 2, pp. 5–6. Quoted from Robert Reid's notes, Shillong Raj Bhavan Records, 9&10.
55. Ibid., n. 2, pp. 5–6.
56. NSF Seminar Paper, n. 2, pp. 6–7.
57. Asoso, n. 9, p. 141.
58. Rammuny, n. 73., p. 21.

CHAPTER THREE

The Naga Resistance Movement

The Naga resistance movement has become a professional military effort, which is targeted effectively. It has also generated much intellectual activity with professional points of view of Naga religious leaders, educator, and social workers generating action ideas which strengthened resistance to Indian rule. The Naga elite behaviour and Naga underground's strategic culture has not seen the "war" as an all out war. The theory and practice of the Resistance both call out for adjustment. The Resistance does not operate in an isolationist intellectual environment; it has room to manoeuvre both in relations with the authorities in India and in the international sphere. It can pursue its overall interests on the basis of real politics as well as the idealistic trends which support the preservation of traditional cultures and advancement of human rights and democratic principles. The real source of anxiety in the Resistance Movement is the fear that the right balance between individual freedom and social and tribal harmony may not be preserved as the larger forces of global economy permeate the Naga soil and economic life. Moreover even if the negotiations are successful it will take many years for the scars of this protracted resistance movement.

A. Emergence of Naga Nationalism

The genesis of the Naga Nationalism could be traced from the first World-War. On the eve of this historic war, nearly 2000 strong Naga tribal men were recruited by the Britishers to serve as the labour corps in the French front in 1917. The separation of this large number of young Naga men from their tribal land had been a unique experience. For the first time in Naga history the Nagas got an opportunity to intermingle with the outside world which they have not experienced before.[1]

However, from the experiences they gained in the war and from their contact with the totally different civilised men, the Naga soldiers came to realise their own ethnic, linguistic, social and cultural uniqueness. This differentiation of Nagas themselves from the others have cleared the way to organise themselves into a small unit called the Naga Club in 1918. The formation of this exclusive ethnic club by the Naga tribe was a significant landmark, which brought the unity and oneness among the various Naga tribes. Thus, the Nagas association with the first World War had enlightened the spirit of the Nagas which spearheaded an upsurge leading to the Naga National Movement.[2]

The Naga National Movement entered into a crucial phase during World-War II. The war helped in bringing about a greater degree of unity and solidarity among the various Naga tribes. Circumstances in the war created situations for few British administrators to lend credence to the growth of Naga National Movement. Sir Charles Pawsey the then Deputy Commissioner of the Naga hills district had displayed an influencing concern over the Nagas. An interesting episode during the British resistance against the Japanese bolstered Pawsey to lend support to the Nagas. The marauding Japanese were pursuing Pawsey in the deadly battle of Kohima in 1944. The Naga villagers relentlessly supported and protected him from the Japanese. Field Marshall Sir William Slim in his book: *Defeat into Victory*, writes:

> The gallant Nagas whose loyalty even in the most depressing times of the invasion has never faltered. Despite floggings, torture, execution and the burning of their villages, they (Nagas) refused to aid the Japanese in any way or to betray our troops. Their active help to us was beyond value or praise. Under the leadership of devoted British political officers, some of the finest types of the

> Indian civil services, in whom they have complete confidence, they guided our columns, collected informations, ambushed enemy patrols, carried our supplies, and brought in our wounded under the heaviest fire. Many a British and Indian soldiers, owe his life to the naked head-hunting Nagas, and no soldiers of the fourteenth army who met them will ever think of them but with admiration and affection.[3]

And further the Japanese defeat was made possible only through the help of the Nagas who "rendered valuable services obsequiously to the allied forces"[4] Sir Andrew Clow, the then Governor of Assam wrote to Governor General of India, Lord Wavell, that " they wanted to help the Nagas who did magnificent work in helping them during the war."[5] As a token of gratitude to the Nagas, Sir Charles Pawsey established an organisation called the Naga Hills District Tribal Council in April 1945 .The major objective of the council was to bring together and unite all the Naga tribes, to help in repairing the damages done during the world war II. However, the Council got transformed into almost potent political organisation known as the Naga National Council (NNC), at the Wokha conference on 2nd February, 1946. Initially, the NNC was confined to catering to the welfare and social aspirations of the Nagas but later extended its field to political activities to achieve the Naga independence from the foreign yoke. Since then the NNC has been active as the main political organ of the Nagas.

The formation of the NNC was a major step which initiated the consolidation of disparate nationalistic force.[6] The NNC elected T. Aliba Imti as President and T. Sakhrie as the General Secretary, to run the NNC office. At its inception the NNC comprised only 29 members representing few tribes.[7] Later on the membership was made compulsory for all the Naga citizens in general and a voluntary contribution of rupee one to hundred or more was collected from each and every family[8] towards the NNC fund. They also enjoyed the patronage of the British administrators, educated Nagas and the salariats. Under the auspices of the NNC, the leadership brought out a regular monthly journal called, the Naga

Nation, published from Kohima... The 'Naga Nation' as the propaganda organ of the NNC, created immense political consciousness and identity. Further it played vital role by educating the Naga tribes about not only their socio-economic problems but also their culture and rich traditions.

The first political move by the NNC was in October 1946. They passed a resolution demanding the Deputy Commissioner of Naga Hills District, to restrict the entry of member of any political party, from the rest of India, into the Naga hills without the consent of the NNC.[9]

The most drastic step of the NNC was its call for the Naga self-determination. But the predicaments were:

1. whether the Naga Hills would be able to constitute an Independent Sovereign State after the British left India; and,
2. whether the Nagas would be able to attain independence and run a Sovereign State.

Over the issue of the Nagas independence, the extremist group led by A.Z. Phizo demanded complete independence, while the moderate group (mostly government servants) favoured the continuance of the relations with the Government of India till the Nagas are in a position to run a modern state. The third group came with the idea of Nagaland as a mandatory state under the British Government (direct control from Britain) for a specific period of time.[10] But majority of the NNC opposed this proposal and feared that the Britishers were bent on colonising their country.

The different opinions were accommodated within the NNC, and as a consequence, the NNC resolved to pass a four-point resolution on 19th June, 1946 at the Wokha conference. These resolutions were submitted to the representative of His Majesty Government (Cabinet Mission).

It reads:

1. At NNC stands for the solidarity of Naga tribes including those in the unadministered areas.
2. This Council strongly protest against the grouping of Assam with Bengal.

3. The Naga hills should be included in Autonomous Assam in free India with local autonomy and due safeguards for the interest of the Nagas.
4. The Naga tribes should have a separate electorate.[11]

But the Cabinet Mission could not take any further decision as demanded by the NNC for the future course of the Nagas. This resolution was sent to Pandit Nehru by two Naga students (T. Sakhrie, NNC Secretary and Sashimeren Aier). Nehru responded to their letter in August 1946, which was not in favour of an independent Nagaland.

He wrote:

> "It is obvious that the Naga territory in eastern Assam is much too small to stand by itself politically or economically. It lies between the two countries India and China and part of it consists of rather backward people who require considerable help. When India is independent as it is bound to be soon it will not be possible for the British government to hold on the Nagas territory or any part of it. They could be isolated between India and China. Inevitably, therefore, this Naga territory must be part of India and Assam with which it has developed such close association."[12]

An Indian scholar has argued with insight that as "India was yet to make its claim over the land of the Naga Hills, and Nehru clearly stating that the Naga territory was too small to exist an independent nation and for strategic reasons it must joint the Indian Union."[13] Nehru contended that the Naga Hills though not a part of India, it was too small to exist as a sovereign state. And as it has not matured both politically and economically, he suggested for its inclusion within Indian territory for its development. Besides, Nehru also saw strategic importance of the Naga Hills.

i) Interim Demand

When the departure of the British from India was imminent, the NNC, after series of discussions over the issue of Nagas complete independence, resolved to request for an Interim Government to look after the Naga Hills for a specific period of time. According to NNC request "the Government of India was to act as the guardian power for a period of ten years at the end of which the Nagas would be free to determine their political future."[14] Then to that effect, they submitted a memorandum to the last Viceroy of India, Lord Louis Mounbatten on 9th April, 1946. The terms proposed for the ten year Interim Government were:

1. "The Interim Government of the Naga people will be a government by the Naga people over all the people of Nagaland, having full power in respect of legislation, executive and judiciary.
2. Nagaland belongs to the Naga people and will be inalienable.
3. The Interim Government of the Naga people will have full power in the matter of raising and expenditure to revenue, and annual subvention to cover the deficit being given by the guardian power.
4. For defence and for aiding civil power in case of emergency a force considered necessary by the NNC will be maintained in Nagaland by the Guardian power. That force will be responsible to the NNC who will in turn be responsible to the guardian power."[15]

However, the British Indian Government could not respond to this appeal except for some vague expression given to the NNC. They were asked to discuss their wishes to the Advisory Committee on the Aboriginal Tribes which would visit Kohima. Perhaps, "Sir Prime Minister Winston Churchill's Conservative party was voted out of power, and the Labour Government did not want any further confrontation in the sub-continent."[16] They lost interest and remained silent on the NNC memorandum.

The ultimate visit of the sub-committee of the Advisory Committee on 20th May, 1947 could not favour for any constitutional arrangements, whereas the Nagas demanded independence, without any outside interference after the end of ten year guardianship.[17] The Advisory Committee wanted the

Naga hills be included within the Indian Union. This led to another stalemate of uncertainty for the vexed Naga national question.

In an attempt to break the impasse, Sir Akbar Hydari, the then Governor of Assam, a "henchman" of Jawaharlal Nehru was sent to Kohima on 27th June, 1947 to impress the Nagas and to understand the realities of the situation.[18] A memorandum submitted to Sir Akbar Hydari by NNC on 26th June 1947 at Kohima, reads: "The Naga National Council stand for solidarity of all the Naga region. The present Naga Hills district had arbitrarily been carved out for administrative convenience."[19] In the presence of Sir Charles Pawsey the discussion was carried on for three days (27 to 29, June 1947) with the NNC; on the issue of Ten Years Interim Demand, after a series of hectic discussions it ended up in the Nine-Point Agreement known as Hydari Agreement.

ii) Hydari Agreement

The Hydari Agreement had been made with the consent of Jawaharlal Nehru. The preamble of the agreement recommended that "the right of the Nagas to develop themselves according to their free expressed wishes is recognised".[20] In other words it was equal to ranging from prevalent tribal laws to the ownership of land and taxation.[21] But clause 9 of the agreement turned controversial between the NNC and the Government of India. The clause 9 of the article runs:

> "The government of Assam as the agent of the government of Indian Union will have a special responsibility for a period of ten years to ensure the due observance of this agreement; and at the end of this period the Naga National Council will be asked whether they require the above agreement to be extended for a further period, or a new agreement regarding the future of the Naga people would be arrived at."[22]

This agreement as the Nagas understand was that after ten years, they would have their sovereign state, whereas the Government of India asserted that it would mean Nagaland remaining a protected state of India even after the expiry of ten years.

The clause 9 of the agreement, however, implanted seeds of discord within the NNC, resulting in their division into the extremists and the moderates. In order to resolve their differences Sir Charles Pawsey persuaded them to put the issue to vote. The moderates (who were mostly government servants)[23] won by a slight majority to accept the agreement. But the extremist group led by A.Z. Phizo strongly protested against the agreement; it does not state that the Nagas would be independent after the end of the ten year period.[24] They thus declared the agreement null and void.

In the middle of their discussions on the agreement, Sir Akbar Hydari warned the Nagas, in the presence of Pawsey and others, that if the Nagas refused to join the Indian Union, India would use force against the Nagas.[25] His policy was to win over the Nagas by threats, but it was considered a big challenge and it only enraged the aspiration of the Nagas.[26] The possibility of Sir Charles Pawsey and P.F. Adams, Secretary of the government of Assam misleading the moderates with the contents of the agreement has also been raised by some sections. The Secretary and Advisor to the Government of Assam, P.F. Adams told "the Nagas to remain with India saying that India would go into pieces within five years. So that the Nagas can get out any time as we would like to be glorified through some downfall."[27] It is argued that the moderates knowledge of language was very limited and they were not politically mature to understand the wording of the controversial clause 9 of the agreement, they hope, would meet the full aspirations of the Nagas for independence.[28] Over the disagreement, the extremist Naga delegation consisting of nine members led by A.Z. Phizo and Kughato Sukhai went to Delhi.

The Naga delegates met Mahatma Gandhi at Bhangi Colony on 19th July, 1947 to plead for the demand of the Nagas. They told him that Nagas are not Indians; from time immemorial Nagaland was a free nation and not an Indian territory, "the Nagas are resolved to declare their independence a day before India would do so on 14th August 1947."[29] The Naga delegates asked for his help to save the Naga hills from India's occupation. Then Mahatma Gandhi told the delegates,

> "Nagas have every right to be independent. We did not want to live under the domination of the British and they are now leaving us. I want you to feel that India is yours. I feel that Naga hills are mine, the matter must stop there. I believe in the brotherhood of man, but I don't believe in forced union. If you do not wish to join the Union of India, nobody forces you to do that." The Naga delegates pointed out that Sir Akbar Hydari was threatening them with the use of force in the event of their refusal to join the Indian Union. Gandhi exclaimed "Sir Akbar is wrong: He can not do that ... I will come to the Naga Hills, I will ask them to shoot me first before one Naga is shot."[30]

The father of the Indian nation had great sympathy and understanding towards the Nagas. He also inspired the Nagas to follow the way of non-violence to decide their future. The Naga delegates returned with great hope given by Gandhi. They hoisted the sovereign "Naga flag" on the 14th of August 1947 and declared Nagaland an independent country. (This date has been observed till today). Telegrams regarding the declaration of independence were sent to the Government of India, foreign Diplomatic Missions in Delhi and a message was sent to the United Nations Secretary General. But the Government of India did not recognise the Nagas independence. The assassination of Gandhi proved a great loss to the Nagas. Had he lived longer the Nagas could possibly have gained independence at that stage. This led the extremist nationalist Nagas resolve to fight till the last for the Nagas self-determination.

In the midst of the Naga political imbroglio, the NNC leadership was divided again. The moderate NNC unanimously decided to modify the controversial clause 9 of the Hydari Agreement and submitted an ultimatum to the Government of India on 4th November, 1947. The new modification of the article reads:

> "The Governor of Assam as the agent of the Government of Indian union will have a special responsibility for a period of ten years to ensure due observance of this agreement. At the end of this period Nagas will be free to decide their own future."[31]

The NNC firmly stood for the modification of the clause 9 of the agreement. That is, if the Government of India did not implement the new modification, the Naga people shall cease to be a part of Indian Union from 6th December, 1947.[32]

This ultimatum was forwarded by Sir Charles Pawsey who did not fully favour the Nagas claim for independence due to the Naga rejection of earlier "crown colony scheme." Instead he recommended over the NNC memoranda that, "at the end of this period the NNC will be free to decide what arrangements will be made for the future administration of the Naga country must remain in the Indian union."[33] He could forsee the shortcomings of the Government of India policy and predicted that the Nagas would not achieve their independence.

The extremist group led by A.Z. Phizo rejected any new arrangement except complete independence. They rejected the modification of the agreement clause 9 which was not fully an aspiration of Naga independence.

The Hydari Agreement remained in abeyance for nearly a year as the Government of India was not serious with the Agreement. Therefore, the NNC delegation called on the Governor Sir Akbar Hydari at Shillong on 22nd July, 1948 to get assurance for the implementation of the agreement. The Governor and Premier of Assam G.N. Bordoloi met the Naga delegates and gave a written assurance that, "there was absolutely no cause for nursing unfounded fears and doubts."[34] But with the sudden death of Sir Akbar Hydari on 28th December, 1948, the 9-point agreement was a discarded paper and it was no longer considered by New Delhi.[35]

It may be pointed out that at the time of the departure of Britishers from India, the Nagas strongly demanded that they should be left alone as they were before to decide their future. But ruefully, the British left the fate of the Nagas in the hands of India and Burma. The argument was that the British colonialists did not have any moral right to hand over the Naga Hills to any country, either Burma or India. British colonialists occupied only some part of the Naga Hills for their administrative convenience. From time immemorial, the Naga Hills were never a part of India and were not subjugated by any alien rulers. So the question of secession from Indian Union did not arise. The Nagas struggle for Independence is purely a resistance movement.

Meanwhile, when Governor-General of India, Shri C. Rajagopalachari visited Shillong on 28th November, 1949, the Naga delegates appraised him of their demand for independence. He realised the ethnic differences of Nagas from the other tribal people and assured the delegates that "Nagas were at full liberty to do as they like either to become part of India or to separate, if they felt it, it would be best in their interest to be isolated."[36] Similar opinion was given by Shri Parkash, the then Governor of Assam on 14th January, 1950. He also acknowledged that the Nagas were at full liberty to remain outside the Indian Union.[37]

Ethnically, Nagas are of the Mongoloid race. The Nagas' demand for sovereignty was considered as genuine demand by many great Indian leaders. It was the Nehru government that forced the Nagas to join the Indian Union against their wishes in deciding their own future.

The Naga nationalist movement entered into a more militant phase when A.Z. Phizo joined the movement in 1946. On his release from Rangoon jail and return to Kohima, the movement became more intensive. Shortly, he withdrew from the NNC due to ideological differences with the NNC moderates in 1948. Then he pursued a more forceful policy and formed 'People Independent League for Sovereign Nagaland' comprising the Naga Hills of Tuensang Frontier Division and contiguous Naga Hills in Assam, Manipur and Burma.[38] But he was arrested in 9th July 1948 on the pretext of his pro-Pakistani's and the anti-Indian propaganda[39] to liberate the Naga Hills from India's occupation. Under the Regulation Act of 1818 he was sent to Presidency Jail in Calcutta but was released unconditionally on 18 December, 1948 after his family met a tragic accident.

iii) Phizo's Personality, Values and Attitudes

Individual political personalities play an important role in the inculcation of attitudes which focus on ethno-nationalism as a vehicle of revolutionary progress. Phizo's personality created a "personal operational code and a value structure" which filled the vacuum left by the British when they withdrew from the Naga Areas. Phizo could transcend the narrow views of local tribal interest and also provide a wide ranging analysis of geopolitical, political, economic and military developments in the region and articulate how the Nagas as an indigenous people perceived the modernisation process in their home region. He served "ethnic, cultural and national-instrumental" interests of the Nagas by providing a sense of common political destiny. If the option of substantial and real autonomy had been given, it is doubtful if he would have rejected it. He reluctantly evolved cogent ideology with the significant dimension of separatist struggle against the Indian Union in reaction to the Indian state machinery's "propaganda and ideological indoctrination" towards which the Naga intelligentsia was not prepared to be submissive or docile. Phizo therefore undertook his important political mission as a "reluctant revolutionary" when he found his way blocked by the framework of the modern territorial state. An ironical angle of this scenario is that the initiation of violence came from a Government which claimed a passionate interest in the project of Gandhian values of non-violence. This paved the way for the role of violence in the Naga ethnic and separatist struggle and peaceful compromise became less and less likely. Nevertheless Phizo reamained at all times prepared for reduction of tensions and promotion of peaceful change. He did not allow prestige and self-righteousness to come in the way of mutually acceptable solutions based on enlightened humanist ideals.

The return of A.Z. Phizo became very significant in the Naga National Movement. He was elected as President of NNC in 1950. This laid the foundation of a Naga National movement dominated by radical Nagas corollary to the idea of sovereign and independent state of Nagaland. The NNC rejected the inclusion of "the Naga hills and the Naga inhabited areas kept under Sixth Scheduled of the Indian Constitution on par with other hill tribes of Assam"[40] which was much against the wishes of the Nagas. This led to the rapid deterioration of the Nagas relations with the government of India.

In defiance of the above arrangement, the NNC issued a Declaration which was reported in the international press as follows:

"The Nagas will become a free nation. The Indian Constitution cannot bind the Nagas. An appeal to the world on Republic Day (January 26) that the Nagas will be given freedom of choice to become independent."[41]

Then the NNC passed a resolution on 16th–18th February, 1950 at Kohima for the further policy thus :

1. No Naga should join the Assam Legislative Assembly or Indian Parliament representing the Nagas.
2. Resolved that anything that is autonomous in character will not be accepted by the Nagas.
3. The aspiration and inspiration of the Nagas to "fight for freedom is through bloodshed. The Nagas are strongly determined to fight constitutionally for the liberation of their motherland."[42]

iv) Nagas Plebiscite

To explore the views and to ascertain the conviction of the people for an independent sovereign Nagaland a plebiscite was conducted on 16th May, 1951 throughout Nagaland. The result of the plebiscite was tabulated and published on 16th March, 1952 under the aegis of A.Z. Phizo, on two basic issues:

"1. Whether they wanted to remain in India or to be a separate independent state, and
2. To repudiate the charge of the Indian Government that the NNC was supported by only a minority of the people."[43]

It was in fact a forgone conclusion favouring a sovereign independent state of Nagaland, with 99.9% opting for Naga independence. Seven thousand men and women were reported to have given their thumbprint. All the villages in the entire Naga hills were visited, signatures and thumbprint were taken and oath were administered in the Naga traditional manner to fight for Naga independence.[44]

The Eastern Nagas could not, however, be brought into the plebiscite owing to the opposition of the Rangoon Government. But morally they supported the stand of NNC which convinced them that Naga people as a whole had opted for independence and it is an "unalterable mandate."[45] The plebiscite-forms which contained the details of the voters (two volumes of thumb impression) were sent to the then President of India, Dr. Rajendra Prasad. He considered the demand of independence as absurd[46] on the ground that it was made by just a handful of Naga people. He refused to see it as a mandate that the 'ethnic Nagas' love for freedom, which still has its ferments even today. There has also been a negative assumption among some writers that the plebiscite was conducted only in some areas.

When Jawaharlal Nehru visited Assam in December 1951, a five man delegation of NNC led by A.Z. Phizo met him at Sylhet (Tezpur). They put forward their desire for liberation and presented the result of the plebiscite.[47] Nehru further said, "I consider freedom very precious. I am sure that the Nagas are as free as I am, in fact more free in a number of ways. For, while I am bound down by all sort of laws, the Nagas are not to some extend bound by such laws and they are governed by their customary laws and usages. In the present context of affairs both in India and in the world it is impossible to consider for a moment, such an absurd demand for independence of the Nagas. It is doubtful whether the Nagas realise the consequences of what they are asking for. For their present demand would lead them to ruin."[48] Hence the Nagas' demand for independence was projected by Nehru as distant from the near future. While Nehru was favouring to workout the issues within the parameters of the Indian constitution; the Nagas were not willing for any adjustment short of independence.

Thereafter the Government of India, without consulting the Nagas, formulated a policy, affecting the transfer of power, (of the "excluded areas" under the 1935 Government of India Act), to the Government of Assam.[49] This subjugative policy adopted by the Government of India complicated the matters for the Nagas. In retaliation, the Nagas boycotted the first General Election of India in 1952.[50] It was a successful demonstration of unity by the Nagas.

On 11th March, 1952, three delegates led by NNC President A.Z. Phizo met the Prime Minister Jawaharlal Nehru in

New Delhi. It turned out to be a stormy meeting. Nehru "while hammering his table with clenched fist said, whether heaven falls or India goes into pieces and blood runs red in the country, whether I am here or anyone else comes, Nagas will not be allowed to be independent."[51] Nehru was extremely irritated with the demand of the Nagas for independence. The Nagas were shocked and depressed by Nehru's attitude. They returned and immediately sought for outside intervention to settle the Naga issue with India. At Mokokchung in April 1952 "The NNC resolved to appeal to the U.N to take the Nagas under a trusteeship for an interim period prior to their assuming full independence."[52]

In December 1952 A.Z. Phizo left for Burma to internationalise the Naga issue and to raise voice to the rest of the world. But the mission was not successful as he was intercepted by the Burmese Police, being found with several documents and sent back to Nagaland. Thus although the NNC was pursuing their struggle for Naga independence through the Gandhian policy of non-violence, their aspirations for independence still remained as elusive as before.

Thus Nehru, speaking in the Lok Sabha on 11th July 1952 dismissed the Nagas demand as completely unwise, impracticable and unacceptable,[53] and rejected any suggestion to visit the Naga hills to see the reality of this situation for himself. Later on however Jawaharlal Nehru and the Burmese Prime Minister U. Nu jointly visited Kohima the capital of Nagaland, accompanied by Mrs. Indira Gandhi, and B.N. Mullick on 30th March, 1953. The NNC were very keen to submit a memorandum and to speak openly in front of the Naga public with Nehru on the desire of the Nagas for independence.[54] But it happened to be an unfortunate incident for both Nehru, U. Nu and the Nagas. The then Deputy Commissioner of Naga Hills, Barkokati, turned down the NNC request and could not allow either any memorandum submitted or to talk personally with Nehru at that particular public meeting. The Naga leaders protested against the Deputy Commissioner and said "if the Prime Minister would not hear us, then we would not hear him either."[55] There the thousand of Nagas who came stage a "walkout from the public meeting when Nehru was about to make his address, except for a few Government servants mostly non-Nagas.[56] The Prime Minister was shocked, and so was U. Nu[57] This was probably the first time Nehru "the darling of the crowds" was effectively being boycotted in a public meeting. The Deputy Commissioner Barkokati through his insensitive observations poured fuel into the minds of the Nagas.

This demonstration led by A.Z. Phizo once again showed the Nagas unity in demanding Independence. Nehru later accused that the Nagas demand for Independence was the handiwork of British administrators and the American Baptist Missionaries. The Chief Minister of Assam Shri B. Medhi also held that the Naga movement for separation from India was an instigation by foreign hands.[58]

Eventually the Government of India ordered the foreign missionaries to leave the Naga Hills. They also banned the monthly newspaper of the NNC, "Naga Nations" in the same year as an anti-India propaganda paper.[59] There Nehru put the blame on the Assam Government for the episode, but the "wrath of Assam Government fell on the NNC"[60] and ordered the arrest of the Naga leaders.

As soon as the foreigners left, the situation became very tense. Rumours widely spread out. The police made a list of suspected NNC leaders to be arrested for the maintenance of law and order.[61] Shortly on the night of 4th April, 1953, Assam police raided the house of T. Sakhri the then Secretary of NNC.[62] Thereafter Viswema, Jakhama, Kighema, Phesama and Khonoma villages were raided, guns were seized and a number of innocent people were arrested as a follow up. Unable to live peacefully, the apprehensive policy adopted by the Government led the Naga leaders to evade arrest and compelled them to go underground, which sowed the seeds of the Insurgency Movement.

B. The Naga Insurgency Movement and the Armed Conflicts

The beginning of Naga National movement was the mooting of ideas to adopt non-violent means to achieve the Naga Independence. Ideologically, armed confrontation was not the NNC policy for the attainment of their aspiration. Till 1952, the movement was peaceful and intended for an amicable settlement. But after Jawaharlal Nehru's visit to Kohima in 1953, the situation deteriorated, where the Assam government resorted to cracking down on the Nagas. This was the turning point of the insurgency movement. Despite the political turmoil in the Naga Hills, the Nationalist Nagas never submitted themselves to the authority. The Naga leaders' campaign to launch a non co-operation movement resulted into non-payment of taxes, withdrawal of teachers and students from school, and in the resignation of Dobashis, Gaonburas and a wide scale boycotts of all government functions.[63] The philosophy of A.Z. Phizo, which mooted the idea of right of "Nations to Self-determination"[64] intensified the Naga National movement to become more forceful, particularly in the light of the people's verdict favouring home rule.

By now any prospect of negotiations with the Government of India was completely belied with the decision of Government to refuse any further discussions on Naga Independence issue. The Congress party president refused to see the Naga leaders.The then president of India, Dr.Rajendra Prasad declined to receive a Naga delegation in December 1953 in New Delhi,[65] which was the last straw to avoid violence.

In 1953, Bimala Challiha, President of the Assam Pradesh Congress visited Naga hills to observe the situation. He made a sincere attempt to find a solution by a political settlement through peaceful means. To break the impasse, he suggested, "since the constitution is changeable, any defect in it could be removed,"[66] to fulfil the aspiration of the Nagas. But the Chief Minister of Assam, Bishnuram Medhi's attitude shattered the chances for restoring normalcy. His attitudes supposed to be bias on the Naga issue aroused " deeper passion and fierce indignation of the Nagas against the Assamese."[67]

The goodwill Mission of Praja Socialist Party (PSP) led by Hareswar Goswami, Bipinlal Das and B.K. Bhattacharjee was sent to the Naga Hills in November 1953. After touring the interiors of Nagaland, they wrote in their report," whether we like or not, it is a fact that the idea of Independence has become popular with the people of the Nagas."[68] They expressed that the Naga issue could be solved through peaceful means. The Speaker of Lok Sabha Mr. G.V. Mavalankar also visited Naga Hills in January 1954. Though he could not support the demand of the Nagas,[69] he, however, appreciated the aspiration of the Naga people and wished for talks and a better understanding between the Nagas and the Government of India to be established.

In an exchange of 'Goodwill Mission', the Naga people visited Assam to eliminate suspicions and misunderstandings in order to avoid violence and bloodshed and to build bridges for Assamese-Naga relationship. But the situation remained tense in the Naga hills. The Naga Nationalists firmly stood for nothing short of Independent Nagaland. The more the Nagas were suppressed and oppressed the more they joined underground. Despite the deliberate policy on the Nagas by the Assam Government, multitude of dedicated young Nagas went underground and "pledged to fight till the last drop of blood to liberate their fatherland."[70]

Within a short period of time, the Naga underground activities extended to the Tuensang Frontier Areas. It was a free Naga Hills unadministered territory during the British rule in India. The first Hongking* or People Sovereign Republic of Nagaland was formed by A.Z. Phizo in September 1954 with the support of Thungti Chang.[71] (Chief of the Chang tribe). Then the Naga underground organised the Youth Wing, Women Wing and Armed Wing to confront any eventuality.

Herewith a major step was initiated by the Government of India. To bring those frontier areas under the direct Indian administrative control, a political officer with a unit of Assam Rifle was posted in Tuensang.[72] They replaced administrators by non-locals, strengthened the police force, set up nine police posts, and declared the problem to be one of 'just law and order.' This policy was against the wishes of the Nagas. It is argued that it was a continuation of 'internal colonialism' by the government of India in the free Naga Hills. Owing to such a policy the NNC revolted against the Government of India for intruding into Naga territory.

Thereafter, Assam Rifles launched a large-scale armed operation in Tuensang Frontier Areas (Free Nagaland). They

---

* Honking means 'get out' in Chang tribal language. It implied to force the Government of India out from Naga Hills.

burnt down villages, Churches, granaries and standing crop[73] to bring the Nagas to submission. In that situation, an incident took place where a Government dak runner, who happened to be the son of a Pangsha Warrior was killed by Yimpang Villagers. The Government accused NNC, but they denied any involvement. In that unadministered areas, the war-like Naga tribes were still practising head-hunting. Keeping in mind their tribal old feud, also added to stir-up the situation.[74]

On account of that incident the Pangsha Villagers took revenge with the help of the Indian Government. They equipped 60 Pangsha warrior with arms, in collaboration with the Assam Rifle troops, and wiped out the whole village, killing 60 men, women and children including three NNC activists on 15th November 1954.[75] It was reported that the "killing lasted for two hours."[76] The Government of India denied any involvement and Prime Minister Nehru presented a report in the parliament which was restricted to the military version, falling short of reality. No impartial enquiry had been conducted and it was reported that an Indian Intelligence Bureau agent instigated the Pangsha Warrior where he was trailing the president of Naga Youth Movement "who happened to be there."[77]

After that episode on 27th November 1954, a "battalion of Armed Forces destroyed the Chingmei Village by bombardment, causing an unknown total of death."[78] They suspected the presence of NNC activists, but the victims were only innocent citizens. Here too, the government never came out with any report other than the military version.

By the beginning of 1955, "lawlessness and violence were flared up in Tuensang Frontier Areas."[79] The joint forces of Assam Rifles and Armed Forces went on rampant operations[80] to subdue the Nagas. In reprisal to that, the 'Naga Home-Guard' under the 'Hongking Government' took up arms to defend their country. They started confronting and attacking police out posts, looting arms and kidnapping the Assam Rifles. This led to full-scale Indo-Naga armed conflicts.

The first fierce-fighting started from Tuensang Frontier Areas (Free Nagaland) on 25 March 1955. In a short period, it spread to the neighbouring areas. The government of India was unable to contain the force of Naga resistance subsequently, they declared Tuensang and Mokokchung to be 'disturbed area' in the name of law and order disturbances.

The two Acts were introduced by Assam Government between 1953–55 to suppress the Naga insurgence:

1. The Assam Maintenance of Public Order (Autonomous District) Act. 1953.
2. Assam Disturbed Area Act, 1955.[81]

But this could not bring any desired changes. Instead the situation went from bad to worse, day by day, violence only begetting violence, committed by Assam Rifle and the Naga rebels. Innocent citizens caught at the cross fire were unable to live peacefully.

Even in such a critical stage, most of the NNC leaders were overground.[82] An NNC delegation led by A.Z. Phizo and four members appealed to the Assam Government on 15th August 1955 to take up the Naga issue. To avoid any violence, they offered their services as a mediator between the Indian Army and the Naga brothers.[83] Hence, the Chief Minister of Assam Shri Bishnuram Medhi and the NNC delegation signed a pact to restrain violence by both sides. But it was not honoured by Medhi, where he published 'leaflets' in which he puts all blame on the NNC for the disturbances.[84] Thus chances of negotiation receded[85] due to the government injustice to the Nagas.

Meanwhile, NNC was passing through a period of internal 'dissension'. Soon a rift developed between the extremists and moderates. The moderates NNC—T. Sakhrie, Jasokie and others—came out openly protesting violence in the Naga Hills. They held a series of secret meetings to remove Phizo from the NNC Presidentship. They also attempted to re-organise the NNC, to work out the Naga problem in a peaceful way. But such plan failed to materialise.[86]

The division of the NNC leaders became a major set-back to the Naga Nationalist Movement. This division within the party enabled an Indian Intelligent Officer S.M. Dutt to came into intimate contact with the moderate NNC leaders. According to B.N. Mullik "their association with S.M. Dutt was extremely valuable from India's point of view."[87]

The rivalries within the NNC had caused the life of T.S. Sakhrie, a brilliant spokesman for the NNC. He was kidnapped by the members of extremist Nagas on 18th January 1956, and murdered brutally in the jungle.[88] It was reported that he was murdered for siding with the Indian Government. This led to the extremists and moderates split for a no-return. Consequent to that, "A.Z. Phizo was charged for treason"[89] by the government of India. Hence he went underground and organised a strong military Armed Wing to revolt against the Indian hegemony. The undeclared war went on extensively through out the Naga Hills. The growing strength of the Naga rebels could not be contained by the Assam Rifle and the Armed Forces. Therefore the Government of India declared the Naga Hills as a whole to be 'disturbed area' on 31st January 1956.[90] Henceforth the Indian Armed Forces replaced the Assam Police since then "atrocities and rapes increase hideously."[91] Mass arrest, beating, tortured, forced labour and burning of villages, became very frequent.

In the midst of the armed confrontation, the NNC set up a Government called the Federal Government of Nagaland' on 22nd March 1956 at Phensinyu Village in the Rengma Area.[92] They hoisted the Naga National Flag and promulgated a constitution (Yehzabo). The preamble of which began- 'Nagaland is a people Sovereign Republic', this has been so from time immemorial.[93] Simultaneously, a military armed wing was formed, known as the 'Naga Home Guard' to defend the country.

The first weapons came from the dumped stock left in the area by the Japanese and the British forces during the Second World War.[94] Some arms were captured from the Indian Security forces. The other indigenous guns made by the Konyak Nagas, Naga Dao and strong short range of spear's were also used by the Naga rebels.

During the intermittent war, the 'Naga Home Guard' were very 'swift and effective'. Indiscriminate killings were carried out by the Indian army on the Nagas. But the "actual casualties inflicted by Indian armies on Naga guerrillas was very slight."[95] It was only the civilians who suffered heavily. The indulgence of orgy of rape, torture and murder by Indian armies and security forces were debated in the Lok Sabha on

23rd August 1956.[96] The late Dr. Lohia, an Indian Socialist M.P after visiting the areas reported that "rape by Indian troops and police was widespread, he was arrested and ex-Inpelled."[97] But Nehru denied the allegation and charge of Indian armies involvement, where "he decline the suggestion of a parliamentary delegation to visit the Naga areas as impractical."[98] It is fact that any press correspondents were 'forbidden' to enter the Naga area.[99]

Sir Pawsey, after visit to the Naga Hills said that the "Indian army behaviour will never be forgiven."[100] The hardship and suffering received from the Naga guerrillas were retaliated to the innocent villagers by the Indian armies. They arrested the "suspected underground or overground and tortured in diverse manner, kept hanging upside down for several hours, kicked with boots, hit with guns butts and subjected to electric shocks, with the intent of taking revenge."[101] And at the same time, the Naga guerrillas also tortured and brutally murdered the Nagas, whom they suspected of helping the Indian Government.[102]

In the process, A.Z. Phizo conceived a bold idea to siege Kohima to make the headquarter of Federal Government. He marched with the "Naga Home Guard" under the command of Tungti chang.[103] At the time, a young Sema Naga called Kaito, a dynamic leader had already organised the 'Naga Safe Guard'.[104] This two combined armed wing[105] planned to attack Kohima from three different directions on 10th June, 1956. They cut off all telephone lines, electricity, water supply and destroyed bridges and roads. They captured most parts of Kohima and "besieged it for three weeks. The Indian armies almost 'suffered defeat' at the hands of the Naga underground. But the situation was not favourable to the Nagas. The final occupation of Kohima on 22nd July 1956, their arms and ammunition had run low, whereas "massive Indian reinforcements" had gathered forced to withdraw the Nagas. Another factor was the tussle of leadership between Tungti Chang and Kaito Sema which weaken their efforts. Kaito Sema wanted to become commander-in-chief but Phizo supported Tungti Chang as his commander-in-chief. However, this act precipitated in the form of Kaito withdrawing himself as the main striking force from the field.[106] This withdrawal of Kaito troops provided the Indian armies and the Assam Rifles a favourable situation to manage a break through towards occupying Kohima. From there the Naga guerrillas were forced to withdraw.

After the debacle of Kohima, the Indian Government more seriously took up to tackle the Naga guerrillas. The Government deployed "more troops and many more Assam Rifles and Armed Battallions in the Naga Hills and Tuensang Frontier Areas."[107] The presence in full strength of the army and security forces was not sufficient to make the Naga rebels to surrender. It was General Thimayya who was the first Indian leader to acknowledge the Naga problem as a political one after meeting with the Kughato Sukhai, the Prime Minister of Naga Federal Government in October 1956. He pointed out that it needs a political solution.[108]

Henceforth, the Nagas Independence issue was not favoured by the Government of India. So the NNC resolved to send Phizo to London to seek foreign help. In December 1956, he slipped out via East Pakistan (Bangladesh) to London to internationalise the Naga issue.

By now the Government of India deliberately adopted a plan to regroup villages to cut off the Naga rebels from the civilians. It was a similar idea of the Britishers against Malaya Communist Guerrillas.[109] The purpose of the regrouping of villages has to break the supplies and intelligent system of Naga underground.

By March 1957, "Villages were herded into groups under dreadful condition."[110] After burning down the villages and granaries they were regrouped into one particular village, called 'concentration camp' fenced round and kept under army protection. They were allowed to go and cultivate their fields within limited hours, and had to come back before the nightfall. It was reported that at that 'concentration camp' because of lack of food, water supply, sanitation and medical care many citizens died of starvation.[111] This was continued for a year.

Then another major step was initiated by raising a force of local militia or village guard to fight against the Naga underground. But this policy forced the Naga rebels to become more defensive. According to B.N. Mullik "There was nearly one security troop to every adult male in the Naga Hills Tuensang area."[112] As a consequence, the Naga Guerrillas also suffered heavily, but did not give up their struggle for freedom.

In the midst of the turbulent atmosphere, S.M. Dutt the Indian Intelligence officer realised that "solution to the Naga problem did not lie only in fighting"[113] with the Naga guerrillas. He conceived a brilliant idea to "separate the Naga Hill District from Assam to form a separate unit. Again he encouraged some of the educated moderate Nagas to settle the Naga issue with the Government of India. By the year end of 1956, the moderate Nagas (break away group from Phizo) formed the Naga Peace Organising Committee.[114] In the meanwhile, the Church leaders also openly came forward and condemned the violence "an appeal to the Christian Nagas to work for peace".[115] As a result of these efforts Naga People Convention (NPC) was formed in August 1957, to bring peace in the Naga Hills. It may be concluded that due to the miserable condition of the innocent civilians, the moderate Nagas and the Church leaders initiated the Peace Move to resolve the Naga problem

The Naga resistance movement can be assessed and evaluated in terms of four distinct themes for developing conflict-resolution approaches:

i) Security Choices and Naga Responses

There is a compelling case for developing responsible and realistic security policies which can turn into real negotiations. The perceived need to consider alternatives is based on the idea that there is need to achieve results which cannot be achieved without a qualitatively new approach. Security patterns are undergoing a change and it is difficult to see how the security logic can remain indefinitely divorced from cross pressures in favour of revival of civil society. As in many other parts of the world the "conflict constellation" is being modified in favour of questions on the political and cultural agenda.

ii) Threat Images within the Naga Resistance

There is ample evidence that the Naga resistance movement also faces the question of maintaining a strong sense of collective identity in the face of fragmentation and competition for political power. New political policy options have to be developed to deal with rivalries between antagonistic Naga formations. What seems evident is that Naga disunity has added to current confusion produced by a collision of political egoisms. Misunderstandings and conflicting interpretation of the Phizo legacy can be serious. Only political dialogue between various Naga groups can provide reasonable expectation for lasting solution.

iii) Balance of Constraints

A pertinent question is whether political instability and endemic violence does not impede socio-economic development and also lead to fissiparous tendencies. A balance of constraint in the Naga resistance movement is essential to gain credibility and adaptational ability.

Different interpretations are possible with the same data stemming from different realms of interest. To obtain an operational consensus care should be taken not to destroy fledgling democratic institutions by falling a prey to self defeating pathologies. The Naga resistance movement should define its core values and central roles to educate the Naga public and not to manipulate it.

iv) Cultural Paradigms and Political Structures

The Naga resistance movement has gone through a sequence of stages and it is necessary to draw attention to different dimensions of the conflict. As the case of South Africa showed that the prerequisite for a successful outcome was that strategies were considered on a "contingency basis, each connected to a specific contextual imperative".

There are far reaching changes occurring in the international system which effect South Asia decision makers. The attainment of realistic goals by the Naga resistance movement requires that Naga leaders to act synergistically to pursue Naga interests. The resistance has demonstrated that Naga cultural institutions are adaptive. The dynamics of conflict and conflict resolution will require "search for innovative cultural paradigm" which can foster new political and economic structures.

REFERENCES

1. Huska Sumi, "The Naga Nationalist Movement", *Seminar Paper* presented at the Sumi Kiphimi Kukhakulu, Nagaland, Jan. 17, 1996, p.
2. Asoso Yonuo,"The Rising Nagas", Published, 1974, Vivek Publishing House, New Delhi, 1979, pp. 125–26, 1974.
3. Ibid., n. 2. quoted from the Field Marshall, William Slims book "Defeat into Victory", p. 148.
4. Ibid., n. 2, p. 160.
5. Huska Sumi, n. 1, p. 2.
6. Udayan Mishra *"North-East India Quest for Identity"*(Naga National Question) Omson Publications, Guwahati, 1988, p. 7.
7. Ibid., n. 6, p. 7.
8. Y. Asoso, n. 2, p. 61.
9. M. Rammuny, *"The World of the Nagas"* Northern Book Centre, New Delhi, 1988, p. 18.
10. A. Alemchiba *"Brief Historical Account of Nagaland"*, The Naga Institute of Culture, Kohima, Nagaland, 1970, p. 169.
11. Y. Asoso, n. 2, pp. 161–62, B. Wati, *Fact and Growth of Naga Nationalism* (Mimeograph), 1993, p. 15.
12. Alemchiba, n. 10, p. 166, M. Ramunny, n. 9, p. 19, Udayan Mishra, n. 6, p. 5, Gaundevia, "War and Peace in Nagaland" Palit and Palit Publishers, New Delhi, 1975, p. 57.
13. Udayan, Mishra n. 6, p. 8.
14. Ibid., n. 6, p. 8.
15. Alemchiba, n. 10, p. 170.
16. NSF Seminar paper, "The Naga Problem—An Account", 14th Dec., 1995, p. 7.
17. The Naga National Rights and Movements, NNC, 1993 (unpublished) p. 35.
18. Y. Asoso, n. 2, p. 171.
19. NNC Memorandum, Kohima, 26 June, 1947.
20. Horam, "Naga Polity"(reprinted, Low Price Publications, Delhi, 1992), p. 13; B. Baboo, The Naga National Movement: An Analysis. *Third World Unity,* Vol. 15–16, March–April, 1979, p. 44.
21. Udayan, Mishra; n. 8, p. 18.
22. The Nine-Point Hydari Agreement, 1947.
23. NNC, n. 17, p. 35.
24. L. Wati, n. 11, p. 28.
25. NNC, n. 17, p. 35; Y. Asoso, n. 2, p. 182.
26. NNC, n. 17, p. 35.
27. n. 17, p. 35.
28. M. Ramunny, n. 9, p. 23.
29. NSF Seminar Paper, n. 16, p. 8.
30. A.Z. Phizo, *"The Fate of the Naga People: An Appeal to the World"*, NNC, 1960 (Unpublished), p. 3.
31. L. Wati, n. 11, p. 30, see also; M. Ramunny, n. 9, p. 27.
32. M. Ramunny, n. 9, p. 27; see also Asoso, n. 2, p. 197.
33. M. Ramunny, n. 9, p. 27.

34. Y. Asoso, n. 2, p. 177.
35. Y. Asoso, n. 2, p. 178.
36. N. Maxwell, India, The Nagas and the North-East, Report No. 17. Revised Edition, Minority Right Group, 1980, p. 5.
37. L. Wati, n. 11, p. 32.
38. Y. Asoso, n. 2, p.
39. M. Ramunny, n. 9, pp. 32–33.
40. B. Baboo, n. 2, p. 44.
41. N. Maxwell, n. 36, p. 5.
42. L. Wati, n. 11, p. 32.
43. M. Alemchiba, n. 10, p. 175; Y. Asoso, n. 2, p. 203.
44. M. Alemchiba, n. 10, p. 175.
45. Y. Asoso, n. 2, p. 202.
46. B. Baboo, n. 20, p. 45.
47. Y. Asoso, n. 2, p. 203.
48. Ibid., n. 2, p. 203.
49. B. Baboo, n. 20, p. 45.
50. Y. Asoso, n. 2, p. 203.
51. N. Maxwell, n. 36, p. 5.
52. Ibid., n. 36, p. 14.
53. Parliamentary Debates, 9 July–11 August, Vol. II, Part I, 1952.
54. Y. Asoso, n. 2, p. 204.
55. L. Wati, n. 11, p. 59.
56. B.N. Mullick, "My Years with Nehru", 1948–64, Allied Publishers, Delhi, 1972, p. 305.
57. Ibid., n. 57, p. 305.
58. N. Maxwell, n. 36, p. 5.
59. Y. Asoso, n. 2, p. 205.
60. Ursula Graham Bower, The Naga Problem (Unpublished Manuscript: 1967), p. 33.
61. Ibid., n. 60, p. 33.
62. Y. Asoso, n. 2, p. 205.
63. Udayan, Mishra; n. 6, p. 9.
64. H.K. Sarin, "Insurgency in North-East India (A Study of Sino-American Role)", Sterling Publishers, Pvt. Ltd., New Delhi, 1980, p. 7.
65. Y. Asoso, n. 2, p. 205.
66. Ibid., p. 209.
67. Ibid., p. 209.
68. L. Wati, n. 11, p. 62.
69. Ibid., p. 62.
70. IWGIA, "The Naga Nation and its Struggle Against Genocide". 1968, p. 25.
71. Y. Asoso, n. 2, p. 211; B. Baboo, n. 2, p. 45; M. Ramunny, n. 9, p. 36.
72. B.N. Mullick, n. 56, pp. 306–7.
73. NSCN Publication, A Brief Political Account of Nagaland" (Manuscript), 1993, pp. 18–20.
74. Y. Asoso, n. 2, p. 211.
75. Huska Sumi, Seminar Paper, n. 1, p. 7.
76. A.Z. Phizo, n. 30, p. 4.
77. M. Ramunny, n. 9, p. 44.

78. A.Z. Phizo, n. 30, p. 4.
79. Y. Asoso, n. 2, p. 212.
80. N. Maxwell, n. 36, p. 6.
81. L. Wati, n. 11, p. 65.
82. Y. Asoso, n. 2, p. 213.
83. A.Z. Phizo, n. 30, p. 4.
84. Ibid., p. 4.
85. U. Mishra, n. 6, p. 10.
86. Y. Asoso, n. 2, p. 213.
87. B.N. Mullick, n. 56, p. 307.
88. Anand, p. 96; Y. Asoso, n. 2, p. 214; M. Ramunny, n. 9, p. 52; Bower, n. 60, p. 41.
89. B. Baboo, n. 20, p. 44.
90. N. Maxwell, n. 36, p. 6; Y. Asoso, n. 2, p. 214.
91. A.Z. Phizo, n. 30, p. 4.
92. Y. Asoso, n. 2, p. 215.
93. Constitution of the Federal Government of Nagaland.
94. Y. Asoso, n. 2, p. 216; N. Maxwell, n. 36, p. 6.
95. Charles Pawsey, "The Naga Problem Confidential Paper", 1965, p. 6.
96. Y. Asoso, n. 2, p. 218.
97. N. Maxwell, n. 36, p. 6.
98. Y. Asoso, n. 2, p. 218.
99. George Patterson, "The Naga Problem" *Journal of the Royal Central Asian Society*, Vol. 50, 1963, p. 332. "Delhi and the Nagas" *Far Eastern Economic Review*, 19 May, 1966, pp. 332–334.
100. Charles Pawsey, n. 95, confidential paper, p. 6.
101. Bertel Lintner, "Land of Jade" (A Journey through Insurgent Burma) Publication, Kiscadale, Bangkok, 1990, p. 42.
102. Charles Pawsey, n. 95, p. 6.
103. B.N. Mullik, n. 56, p. 311.
104. M. Ramunny, n. 9, p. 52.
105. The combined arm wing, 'The Naga Home Guard' and the 'Naga Safe Guard' finally changed the name in 1959, into the 'Naga Army.' U.G, The Naga Problem, 1967.
106. B.N. Mullik, n. 56, p. 311.
107. Ibid., p. 312.
108. Huska Sumi, n. 1, p. 7.
109. B.N. Mullik, n. 56, p. 312; see Ramunny, n. 9, p. 71.
110. Charles Pawsey, n. 95, p. 6.
111. L. Wati, n. 11, pp. 68–71.
112. B.N. Mullik, n. 56, pp. 313–14.
113. Ibid., p. 314.
114. V.K. Sarin, n. 64, p. 139.
115. Alemchiba, n. 10, p. 186; see Gundevia, n. 12, p. 70.

CHAPTER FOUR

Peace Initiative vis-a-vis Creation of Statehood

A. Creation of Statehood

Peace is the ultimate goal of violence. The undeclared war, since early 1955 between the Naga underground and the Indian army, throughout the Naga Hills—led to loss of lives, devastated property, villages, untold suffering and misery of the innocent citizens.[1] By seeing that the Church leaders called upon the Naga underground leaders to settle the on- going Naga problem in a peaceful way. By then, the common people sick of blood-shed yearned for peace and order in the Naga Hills.

In the early part of 1957, a church leaders meeting at Kohima and Impur, sent out appeal for peace.[2] Meanwhile, the so called moderate Nagas came forward. Its aim is to oppose violence and to restore peace and order and to win over the Naga rebels. This group formed a "Reforming Committee" of Naga National Council[3] without the knowledge of underground 'Naga Federal Government' to negotiate with the government of India. The committee elected three candidates to fill the three Assam Legislative Assembly seats, it was uncontested. That was the first time the Nagas participated in the second general election of India in 1957. But they left after the creation of Naga Hills as separate unit in 1957.

From the middle of 1956, the break away group of NNC—the moderate Nagas—rallied themselves and wrote to Prime Minister Jawaharlal Nehru to settle the Naga problem within the Indian Constitution.[4] At the out set, the Intelligent Bureau S.M. Dutt also conceived the idea of encouraging the educated and the moderates Nagas to convene all tribal conference. His motives was to divide the Nagas underground and overground. It was a difficult task, restricted by the Naga underground, but he however managed to convince the moderates Nagas to held the tribal conference on 27th July 1957, represented by Eight tribes.[5] This meeting resolved to call all tribal Naga people convention (NPC) in 1957.

Accordingly, the first all tribal Naga People Convention (NPC) was called at Kohima on 22nd to 26th August 1957, under the Chairmanship of Dr. Imkongliba Ao. It was attended by 1,765 people of different Naga tribes from Naga Hills and Tuensang area of NEFA and 2,000 observers from the other Naga areas.[6] The underground Nagas did not take part, inspite of their initial support. It was not a political party. The objectives of the conference was to act as an 'intermediary' between the underground Federal Government of Nagaland and the Government of India to settle the Naga political problem.[7]

After five days of discussion, the Conference advocated to resolve; (a) "settlement of the Naga issue through negotiation and pending a final political solution"; and (b) "the then Naga hills District of Assam and Tuensang Division of NEFA be constituted into a single Administrative unit under the External Affairs Ministry".[8] This resolution was considered only as an 'Interim arrangement'. The final political settlement were carried out through the Naga underground leaders who joined hand with the NPC to negotiate with the government of India.[9] But the issue of the settlement 'within the Indian Union' was strongly objected to the Naga Federal Government.

However, the Convention resolved to send a nine man delegation headed by Dr. Imkongliba Ao on 27th September 1957 to meet the Governor of Assam, as well as the Prime Minister of India to present their resolution. The Prime Minister Nehru accepted the NPC resolution. On 1st December

1957 as the NPC desired, the Naga Hills Tuensang Area (NHTA) was formed and placed directly under the Ministry of External Affairs. Thereafter the degrouping of villages was undertaken and general amnesty was also granted.[10]

To the moderate Nagas, this was a great step forward for consolidation of the Naga nationalism, but it was not acceptable to the Naga Federal Government.[11] Though instead of acting as a mediator the NPC betrayed the Naga Federal Government. Therefore, the Naga Federal Government charged the "NPC leaders as being puppet of the Indian Government."[12] In defiance of the convention resolution, the underground Nagas, instead of giving up their stance, they "rather chose to continue to fight, adopted a guerrilla war tactic 'hit and run' prowling in small groups."[13]

Despite the threat and protest from the underground Nagas, the second NPC Conference was able to held from 21st to 23rd May 1958 at Ungma Village,[14] attended by 2,705 delegates from various Naga tribes. The Convention endorsed the first NPC resolution and appointed a Liaison Committee consisting of eight members to contact the Naga Underground leaders for bringing a peaceful solution to the Naga political problem.[15] Herewith, the underground leaders came forward insisting that "Government of India should recognise the Federal Government of Nagaland and accept the demand for Independence as a basis of negotiation."[16] Keeping aside the Naga underground request, the NPC leaders went ahead with their own plan for a solution of the Naga problem."[17] They appointed a 'drafting committee'* which "thrashed out 16-point of demand culminating in the decision to establish a Nagaland state within the Indian Union."[18] This was put forward to discuss on the third Naga People Convention which was held at Mokokchung from 22nd to 26th October 1959, attended by 3000 delegates.[19] After much deliberation at the conference the draft was formally approved. But the Federal Government of Nagaland opposed the NPC resolution terming it as a compromise. In pursuance of the NPC resolution the draft was formally presented to the Governor of Assam in

* The draft was signed by the President Dr. Imkongliba; Secretary Mr. Jasokie; Vice President, Mr. Vizol and Joint Secretary, Mr. S. Chubatoshi Jamir.

April 1960 at Shillong. Then later, a delegation comprising 15 Naga leaders headed by the president of NPC Dr. Imkongliba Ao went to New Delhi on 26th July 1960. The talks were carried out with the senior official of the External Affairs Ministry and with the Prime Minister Nehru from 27th to 28th July 1960 for the establishment of the separate Nagaland state within the Indian Union. Except a few modification, the 16-point demand were accepted by the Government of India.[20] In the light of the discussion with the Prime Minister Nehru, the NPC president Dr. Imkongliba Ao pointed out that "the mass of the Nagas favoured complete separation from India, but in view of the practicalities of the solution they were prepared to accept less."[21] True, it was due to pressure from the NPC leader that "the Government of India finally forced to concede statehood for Nagaland within the Indian Union under the jurisdiction of the Ministry of External Affairs."[22] On 1st August 1960, Nehru announced in the Lok Sabha" a new state to be called 'Nagaland' comprising the territory of the existing Naga Hills and the Tuensang Area—the Governor of Assam was to be the Governor of Nagaland."[23] Then a transitional period was arranged during which an 'Interim body' for these years to be constituted consisted of 45 elected members with representative from various tribes in Nagaland.

Meanwhile, the NNC President A.Z. Phizo arrived in London from Zurich (Switzerland) in 1960 to present the Naga case to the West. From 1958 the Nagas had approached Reverend Michael Scott, hero of South West Africa, hoping that he could help the Nagas problem, whom the Nagas saw as a champion of the oppressed."[24] His sympathetic and interest on the Naga issue helped Phizo to get into London, "providing him with office space and services at the African bureau in London."[25] On 30th July 1960 A.Z. Phizo denounced the New Delhi—NPC Pact from London saying that,

> "The Naga struggle was for a complete Sovereign Independent Naga State having international recognition and which at best could have treaty relations with India on the basis of equality and reciprocity and added that the leaders of the NPC who signed for the Naga State in India was a puppet assembly and no agreement could be

> recognised regarding the future of Nagaland except with those people who were fighting and were the true representatives of the Naga Nation."[26]

Henceforth, the Naga guerrillas re-organised again into a stronger and more efficient force, funds were raised, more people recruited both in the army and the civil wings and they began to seek arm aid and support from the neighbouring countries.[27] That was the beginning of the Nagas' political movement entering into the international alignment.

During this time the Indian government refused to allow any foreign correspondent into Naga hills. However, Phizo presence in London had widely focused the press attention on the Naga problem. It was only by December 1960, the Indian government organised a press visit to Nagaland, "consisting of six Indian and five foreign correspondents under an official escort."[28] Although the visit was described as "ludicrous," the "foreign correspondents were carefully shepherded on an arranged tour".[29] They were largely limited to Kohima and could not move freely nor talk as they liked to the people[30] to keep out of touch with the nationalist Nagas which were fighting for Independence.

The foreign correspondent Nevellie Maxwell after a brief tour in Nagaland reported to the London newspaper, *'The Times'* that:

> "Inspite of this frustration i.e. the limitation placed on the correspondents enquiries one conclusion can be drawn: the Naga people desire the greatest possible degree of Independence from India or from anyone else. Some people have now been convinced that sovereignty for this little is simply not feasible, quite apart from the destructive effects its secession would have on the Indian Union and with varying enthusiasm are working to establish Nagaland as a State within India; others—and many more than there are actually under arms—have still not been conceived and remained determined to obtain sovereignty. The difference between the two groups is essentially one of degree and of means, but it has been widened by the savageries of guerrilla campaign...."[31]

In early part of 1961, the English journalist Gavin Young had entered from the back door into the Naga Federal Government territory, arranged by Phizo from London.[32] He was entirely undetected by the Indian army and moved freely among the Nagas. Later London newspaper *'The Observer'*, published four series of his articles about the Indian armies' activities in the Naga hills.[33] He was the first foreign journalist who was able to have contact with the underground Naga Federal Government. After his brief visit he concluded that the Naga underground were strongly supported by the masses favouring Independent Nagaland.

Despite the disagreement with the 16-point agreement, the NFG was forced to launch a more offensive force against the Indian armies. As their activities stepped up, attack on military posts multiplied. The NFG activities were extended to the Naga inhabited areas of Assam, Manipur and Burma in order to seek shelter against the increasing Indian military operations.[34] Till 1961 the Indian army continued the military operation throughout the Naga hills. During this period many NPC leaders were living under the threat of the NFG guerrillas. On 26th August 1961, the main architect of the NPC Dr Imkongliba Ao was assassinated by the Naga underground who rejected the New Delhi-NPC pact and termed the NPC members involving in the said pact as a traitor to Naga Nation.

Indeed, it generated the "division" and animosity in the rank and file of the Naga political movement."[35] Henceforth, the Government of India which had accepted the NPC proposal 'on principle' over reacted itself[36] in favour to the creation of Nagaland state under the Indian constitution. By September 1962, the State of Nagaland Act was passed by the Parliament which provided for the formation of the 16th State of Indian Union.

At this time A.Z. Phizo initiated a peaceful dialogue with the Government of India through Reverend Michael Scott. He made a proposal for cease-fire by both sides. But it was rejected by Nehru. The Government of India maintained that "it was dealing with a handful of armed `miscreants`—almost dacoits— legitimizing the violence."[37] The NPC leaders also held the same attitude and opposed any 'cease-fire' proposal by Phizo.[38] Thus the Government of India replied to Phizo that in order to consider the cease-fire proposal the Naga rebels should "cease hostilities and surrender their weapons."[39] However resenting to the Government of India's demand, Phizo, "stated in London on 8th May 1963 that the demand for "unconditional surrender" "was unacceptable."[40]

On 1st December 1963, the President of India Dr. Radhakrishnan officially inaugurated the State of Nagaland as the 16th State of Indian Union. But this state of Nagaland constituted only a part of Naga hills. A major portion of the population and the areas are outside the Nagaland state. It can be said that the policy of divide and rule was applied by the Government of India which was succeeded to the Nagas and it was succeeded in splitting the contiguous Naga territory into five administrative units. This created a situation, in which Nagas live in four different States in India, viz, Nagaland, Manipur, Arunachal and Assam and one unit in Burma. At present there are 36 Naga tribes in India, out of which 14 tribes are in Nagaland, 17 tribes in Manipur, 3 tribes in Arunachal Pradesh and 2 tribes in Assam. It was a victory over the Naga underground. However, on the other hand, it also invited more complication to the Government of India as well as to the Nagas. Thus the Naga political movement was not for creation of a separate state within India but for total independent country for the Nagas. By the creation of a new state for the Nagas, it has implicated both for India and Burma geographically and politically as well.

B. The Peace Process

The creation of Nagaland State in 1st December 1963 could not bring any solution to the Naga political problem. Instead, the Nagas were scattered to live in different states in India and in Myanmar (Burma) as well. It is argued that Nagaland state has been created by some few educated Naga elites for their political gain. Contrary to the unfulfilment of the NNC aspiration, the violence persisted again. This continuation of hostilities between the Indian Security Force and the Naga Federal Army has created more doubt and suffering of the innocent people.

At this juncture, Reverend Michael Scott,[41] on request from Phizo who lived in London came to India twice: on 21st February and 4th April 1963. He met Prime Minister Jawaharlal Nehru on both the occasions. He discussed the Naga problem with him to work out any possibility of 'cease fire' to bring peace to the Naga people, as proposed by Phizo through Michael Scott from London.[42] Meanwhile, concerned with the turbulent situation in Nagaland state, the Nagaland Baptist Church Council held a convention at Wokha from January 31st to February 2nd 1964. It was attended by more than five thousand Naga people. This convention unanimously resolved to request the Government of India and the Federal Government of Nagaland to form a 'Peace Mission'. Ultimately, the convention nominated Shri B.P. Chaliha (the then Chief Minister of Assam), Jaya Prarkash Narayan (The noted Sarvodaya leader) Shankarrao Deo and the Reverend Michael Scott (A British Citizen). Shankarrao Deo could not join in the mission on health ground. Thus the three members of Peace Mission (which was acceptable to all the sections) was formed. They constituted a peace centre at Chedema near Kohima.

The inclusion of Rev. Michael Scott in the Peace Mission was a tremendous morale booster for the Nagas. His inclusion as the 'International Observer' reflects internationalisation of the Naga case.[43] Enlightened by this, several numbers of educated Nagas joined the underground movement.

The first task of the Peace Mission was to bring about the cessation of hostilities and then to the negotiation for the political settlement. However, after two months of formidable negotiations by the Peace Mission a 'cease fire' agreement was signed on 24th May 1964,[44] at Sakrabama village by the three members of the Peace Mission and Six members on behalf of the Federal Government of Nagaland.[45] The Underground Nagas also insisted on extending the cease fire agreement to all the Nagas inhabited areas such as Manipur, Assam and NEFA. But the proposal came into effect only at three areas of Manipur, Mao, Tamenglong and Ukhrul, which were included in the cease fire arrangement terms.[46] The detailed of the cease-fire arrangement was rectified in August. Then military operation by both the Indian security forces and the Nagas underground ceased from midnight on 5th September. The

Nagas celebrated with "bonfire singing and dancing in the streets and worship in the Churches."[47] This agreement came into effect on 6th September 1964.

The cease-fire agreement is made, "on the understanding that security forces of the Government of India undertake to suspend jungle operation, searches of villages, aerial actions, arrests and imposition of political fines and force labour". On the other hand "The Federal Government also undertook to suspend, snipping and ambushing, imposition of fines, kidnapping, recruitment, sabotage, raids and firing security posts, town and administrative centre and moving with arms in uniform in towns, villages and administrative centre and 1000 yards away from security post."[48] It was also agreed that the Indian security forces would patrol to a depth of 3 miles as the crow flies from border line and 100 yards on either side of the road.[49] Further the underground Nagas Federal Government also gave assurance that no arms would be imported from abroad during the time of cease-fire.[50]

Initially, the cease-fire agreement was for one month, but it was extended from time to time until 15th October 1965. So to co-ordinate and ensure successful implementation of the cease-fire agreement, a four member Peace Observer Team was appointed by the Peace Mission with the approval of the Government of India and the Federal Government of Nagaland. Team members were: Shri Nabakrishna Choudhury, Dr. M. Aram, Santi Amalprabha Das and Miss Marjorie Sykes.[51] This team was authorised to investigate any allegation of cease-fire violations but they were not to investigate allegations or complaints prior to 24th February 1965.[52]

Once the cessation of hostilities had been finalised by both the parties, the cease-fire came into force. This led to open the political negotiation to resolve the Indo-Naga Armed Conflict (Naga political question).

i) Peace Talks

The first ever Indo-Naga Peace Talks was started on 23rd September 1964 at Chedema Peace Camp near Kohima. The talks were held in two phases. At the Governmental level, Y. Gundevia the Foreign Secretary led the official delegation, and Zashi Huire, the underground leader led the Naga Federal Government. While welcoming the holding of talks, Gundevia reaffirmed that any political settlement of the Naga problem should be within the framework of the Indian Constitution. But responding to the speech, the underground leader Zashi Huire pointed out that Nagaland was an 'Independent Country' and he expressed that the "Nagas would never yield to Indian Government efforts to 'subjugate' their country."[53] He "called upon India to contribute to the establishment of peace in this part of South East Asia."[54] From the beginning of the Peace Talks it had become a dead locked. After five more round of talks there was no concrete understanding to work out the vexed Naga problem. The reason behind the stalemate was the Naga Federal Government refused to accept "Nagaland Constitution Status" within the Indian union, and its assertion for the rights to self-determination and sovereign Nagaland State[55] which was not acceptable to the Government of India.

To overcome the obstacle of the peace talks, the Peace mission came out with a new proposal that the "NFG could on their own volition decide to be a participant in the Union of India and mutually settle the terms and conditions for that purpose. On the other hand, the Government of India could consider to what extent the pattern and structure of the relationship between Nagaland and the Government of India should be adopted and recast so as to satisfy the political aspirations of all sections of Naga opinion."[56]

Again this proposal ended up in a dilemma. The Government of India welcomed this proposal "to join the Nagaland in the Union of India on their own volition." It is argued that behind this proposal the intention was to give more autonomy to Nagaland states. But it was not clearly mentioned to what status the Government of India would consider this proposal. It was rejected again by the NFG. Instead they demanded another 'plebiscite' under the neutral body supervision[57] to join the Indian Union and to decide their future according to 'their own volition.' But the NFG demand was not accepted by the Peace Mission as well as the Government of India. Since there was no meeting place between the two sides, the Peace Mission proposal was considered by the NFG as a basis for future negotiations. The Naga Federal leaders referred the Peace Mission to discuss their proposal with the Tatar Hoho (the Supreme NFG Parliament). However, there was no proper response from the Tatar Hoho. Instead, they demanded the negotiation to be upgraded to the higher level. Consequently, the Peace Mission urged both the Government to meet at the 'Prime Ministerial level' to discuss the crux of the problem.

ii) The Ministerial Talk

The first round of Ministerial talks between the Prime Minister, Smt. Indira Gandhi and the Naga Federal leaders led by Kughato Sema,* Ato Kilonser (Prime minister) was held in New Delhi on 18 February, 1966 in the presence of Peace Mission. There were six round of talks. The first round did not yield any results. They exchanged their views and discussed the grave situation of the cross violation of cease-fire agreement by both the parties in Assam and Ukhrul district in Manipur. Again they agreed to continue to talk at the same level. But at this critical juncture, the Peace Mission was dissolved. J.P. Narayan had resigned on 25th February, 1966, on the ground that the Federal Naga leaders had 'no confidence in him.[58] After two months, Reverend Michael Scott who was relentlessly working for the Peace Mission was ordered to leave India, blaming on the ground that he was 'soft and partisan' with the Nagas. On 3 May, 1966, the Indian Government ordered his deportation from the country, seized 'all his recording and papers.'[59] Then, B.P. Chalila, lone member of the Peace Mission, was forced to quit from the Mission on 4 May, 1966 after the sabotages of train in Lumding** by the Naga army.[60]

However the Peace talks was not broken off, hoping for some Peace solution. At the fourth round of talks, Smt. Indira Gandhi stated that "solution need not be found with the framework of the Indian constitution" but 'within the Indian

* The NFG delegates who were participating in the talks were, Kughato Sema, Prime Minister Imkongmeren Ao, Vice-President NNC, Isak Swu, Foreign Secretary, S. Angami, Secretary to the Ato Kilonser, CPM, Toshi Chase, Secretary to the Peace Mission, Dalinamo, Press Move, Naga Federal Government.

** Lumding is one of the railway station in Assam.

union', meaning "constitution could be amended in a way to obtain the solution of the Naga problem."[61] This was regarded as a compromising formula from the Government of India point of view to give 'autonomous status' (protectorate) to Nagaland, while the Naga Federal leaders continued their insistence on sovereign and independent Nagaland. To consider the Government of India proposal, the NFG sought to consult the President of NNC, A.Z. Phizo, from London. But he seemed adamant, stating that, "as long as the Indian talk and think in terms of 'special status' for Nagaland within the union of India we do not expect any good thing to come out. What is needed is third party to help both the countries."[62] The next two round of talks were futile meetings, as both the sides remained too rigid to break the stalemate. This led to a deadlock of the Peace talks. On the eve of Nagà Federal leader's departure, from Delhi, Z. Ramyo said to the pressmen at Delhi airport that, "it is for India to treat us either as friend or throw us to the other side." The Vice-President of NNC, Mr. Imkongmeren Ao, also issued a statement after their return to Nagaland that "so far as the talks are concerned, they are finish, and India was responsible for the failure. Now we have to act according to circumstances."[63] The argument is that the dissolving of the Peace Mission was foredoomed to failure of the Peace talks. There was no mediator for the negotiations and to bring to the compromising solution.

As a consequence of the failure of the peace talks the NFG apex body, the Tatar Hoho (Naga Federal Parliament) and the members of the Parliament wrongly blamed Kughato Sukhai for the failure of the talks. Though, without any justification "no confidence' was moved by Tatar Hoho against his leadership. Consequently, he resigned from the Ato Kilonser (Prime Minister) on 24 October, 1967.[64] Since then there was sudden changes in political leadership in the Naga Federal Government. General Kaito Sema, who was one time Defence Minister and later became a member of Tatar Hoho was also ousted.[65] Scato Swu resigned from the post of President. He was replaced by Mahiashieu relatives of Phizo and General Mowu Angami was appointed the Naga Federal Army General. Th. Muivah (Tangkhul Naga) was appointed as General Secretary and Z. Ramyo (Tanghul Naga) as Home Minister of the Naga Federal Government.[66] This change of leadership had developed the crack within the Naga National Movement. The hegemony of Sema leadership was overthrown by the Angami Nagas and the Tangkhul Nagas. This trend suggested tribalism has appeared in the Naga National Movement. It is indicative of the nature of politics that some had the inclination to take the credit of the Movement. In that pursued this political 'entrepreneur' devise strategy and manipulate symbols was based on the lines of tribalism and regionalism.

Herewith, General Kaito, broke away from NFG and "organised stronghold in Sema territory in June, 1967" and formed the 'Revolutionary Government of Nagaland'. It was not only the Sema group that broke away from NFG but even Les Chino of Puchery Naga tribes, Hopong Yimchunger Naga and Thungti Chang from Tuensang joined the Revolutionary Government. The leadership crisis within the NFG did major damage to the Naga National Movement. Within a short period, General Kaito Sema, was assassinated on 3 August 1968, in the heart of the Kohima market by the Naga Federal army. There was strong allegation that he had links with the Indian Armies. It also appeared that Kaito Sema was assassinated for being pro-establishment who had developed ambition against the interest of the NFG.[67] By retaliating to the Kaito assassination, the Revolutionary group General Zuheto kidnapped the NFG President Mahiashieu, the Secretary to the President Ramyo and Kohevi the Cabinet Secretary of the Federal Government. They released these three federal leaders after bargaining to bring more NFG leaders but with not much success. It was reported that this Revolutionary Government had worked jointly with the Indian security forces to capture the Naga Federal Army. The NFG and the NNC denounced the formation of Revolutionary Government and labelled them as 'renegades and traitors' and refused to grant them recognition.[68] At this time of uncertainties, the Naga Federal Army led by General Mowu and Isak Swu returned from China in 1969, with the heavy sophisticated arms.[69] Without having any knowledge of the crisis within the NFG, General Mowu reached Phesami camp (NFG camp) with 165 soldiers of Naga Federal Army, but were captured by the Indian security forces with the help of the Revolutionary group. None of the soldiers were able to escape. They were forced to surrender and deposit their arms in three instalments on 20, 22 and 30 March.[70] Then again Isak Swu and his group of 124 Naga Federal Army which had entered Nagaland through Tuensang district were also captured by the Indian security forces with the help of the Naga village guard.[71] But Isak Swu managed to escape. All this plan had been done by the Revolutionary Government in collaboration with the Indian security forces. This was a great moral booster for the Government of India. But for NFG, it was a great loss, surrendering all the arms with the able fighting forces trained from China.

The splits within the NFG, had also deeply affected the ruling NNO (Naga National Organisation) Government in Nagaland state. The dissidents led by Chubatoshi Jamir (S.C. Jamir in short) challenged the Chief Minister Hokishi Sema leadership for patronising the Revolutionary Government. Soon, they defected from NNO and joined the UDF (United Democratic Front) which was a pro-Naga Federal Government. It was said that the then Chief Minister Hokishi Sema patronised the Revolutionary groups on the understanding to settle the Naga problem with the Government of India.[72]

At this time of political crisis within the parties in Nagaland state, an attempt was made to assassinate the Chief Minister Hokishi Sema on 8 August, 1972 by the Naga Federal Army. But he escaped miraculously unhurt. The Nagas in general strongly believed that the attempt to eliminate him was made on the following grounds:

1. He was shortly due to attend a UN Conference as a member of the Indian delegation. This might have seen as a big threat to the cause of Nagas independence.
2. He was wooing the Revolutionary Government for a separate settlement with the Indian Government,[73] and
3. The transfer of Nagaland from the External Ministry to the Home Ministry.[74]

Subsequent to the incident, the Indian Army was called back into action and the Government of India terminated the extension of 8 years cease-fire agreement on 1 September, 1972.

This was followed by the Unlawful Activities Prevention Act, 1967 enforced in Nagaland; it also re-instituted the Armed Forces (Special Power) Regulation,[75] and the NFG, Naga Federal Army, and NNC were banned as unlawful organisations.[76] The Nationalist supporter, were also threatened of action by Governor, if any body preached 'Secession'.[77]

Ever since the formation of Revolutionary Government, struggle to win the support and confidence of the Naga people. They planned to negotiate with the Government of India and asked for the 'Protectorate' within Indian union. In fact, they wanted like the 'status of Sikkim' but the Governor refused the proposal.[78] But finally, understanding with Hokishe Sema, the then Chief Minister of Nagaland, an arrangement was made for their surrender. Consequently, on 16 August 1973, 1500 persons surrendered along with arms at Zuneboto in front of B.K. Nehru the then Governor of Nagaland.[79] The Prime Minister also "sanctioned Rs. 25 lakhs for the rehabilitation of these people."[80] Moreover, most were taken into the BSF with Zuheto becoming a commanding officer; Mr. Zekheyi was made a Deputy Commandant. The President of India, nominated Scatu Swu, the leader of the group as a member of the Rajya Sabha.[81]

After this event in the middle of 1973, the situation in Nagaland deteriorated again. The Indian Armed Forces launched extensive operations[82] against the Naga Underground. In retaliation, the Naga Federal Army also took counter measures against the Indian Armies. Eventually the situation got more deteriorated and went from bad to worse as before. This was a period when many cadres of Naga Federal Armies who successfully went to China for military training returned with sophisticated arms. Perhaps, the Nagas' connection with China was big threat to the Government of India. This had mounted more pressure on the Government of India to restrict the Nagas' Underground activities. Thus a lot more atrocities were committed against the civilians. On account of the prevailing situation in Nagaland the Church leaders came into the Naga political scenario. To bring both the parties to negotiation, they appointed a liason committee to persuade the Naga underground leaders as well as the Government of India. After months of works by the Liason

Committee,* finally an understanding for peaceful negotiation was reached between the Naga underground leaders and the Government of India. To negotiate with the Government of India the President of the Naga Underground Federal Government, Zashi Huire appointed six members of Federal and NNC representatives[83] led by Kevie Yalley (Phizo's brother).**

The representatives of the Federal and NNC met the Governor of Nagaland L.P. Singh who represented the Government of India, on 10 and 11 November 1975 at Raj Bhavan, Shillong (capital of Meghalaya). After serious discussions the two parties formally entered into agreement on 11 November 1975 which is known as Shillong Accord.

C. The Shillong Accord (1975)

The points of agreement were:

i) The representatives of the Underground Organisations conveyed their decision of their own volition to accept without condition the Constitution of India;
ii) It was agreed that the arms now underground would be brought out and deposited at appointed places. Details for giving effect to this agreement will be work out between them and representative of the Government, the security forces, and the member of the Liaison Committee.
iii) It was agreed that the representatives of the underground organisations should have reasonable time to formulate their issues for discussion on final settlement.[84]

In fact, while signing the Accord, Veenyiyi Rakhu, one of the representatives of the Federal-NNC refused to be a party to the Accord.[85] It was reported that out of the six representatives, five were compelled to sign the Accord under the circumstances.

After signing the Accord, the Indian Security Forces halted military operations, lifted curfew and released the political

* The Liaison Committee was formed on 5th February 1975 by the Nagaland Peace Council with Rev. Longri A, Kenneth Karluo, Klungshim Shaiza, Dr, Aram and L. Lungalang.

** The Federal and NNC delegates which participated for the talk are, Maj. M. Asa, Z. Ramyo, Dahru, Kevi Yalley Venmiyi Rakzu and I. Temjenba.

prisoners who accepted the Accord.[86] Then the Government of India gave reasonable time to the Naga underground to formulate the other issue for the final settlement. With regards to Clause II of the Agreement, the underground deposited their arms at the Transit Peace Camp at Kohima. This was set up after the Shillong Accord. But Clause I and III of the agreement remained unimplemented. Although, the Shillong Accord of 1975 was taken by the Government of India to be a great breakthrough to the final political settlement and the end of the Naga Insurgency Movement,[87] nevertheless, the Naga people in general and the NNC leaders overseas did not agree to endorse the Accord.

Meanwhile, three Naga delegates* proceeded to London in January 1977 to discuss the matter with the President of the NNC, A.Z. Phizo, but he had given no recognition to the Accord and to the extent of calling the signatories as 'puppets.'[88]

Later, on 14 June 1977, Phizo met the Prime Minister of India, Shri Morarji Desai in London. He wanted a discussion of the Naga problem with the Prime Minister but Morarji Desai declined to go for further discussion on the Naga issue. Saying "if you want to persist on independence, I will have nothing to talk."[89] Indeed, the chances of discussion came to a standstill.

Further, the Shillong Accord created more complication within the Naga underground leaders. In fact, this has brought disunity, misunderstanding and differences of opinion within the Nagas. There were few top NNC leaders abroad who along with those from the Eastern sector of Nagaland widely condemned the Accord. After hearing the news of the agreement Isak and Th. Muivah who were on "Goodwill Mission" to China[90] immediately "denounced the Accord as treason and the signatories representing NNC-Federal Government were declared as traitors."[91] In this connection, seven Naga

---

* Request by the ex-underground organisation, the Government of India agreed to send two ex- underground leaders Shri.Z. Ramyo and Shri Kevi Yalley, and from the Nagaland Peace Council also represented Shri.Kenneth Kerhua to London for the final settlement of the agrrement. But the London Mission returned with failure, the great hopes were in vain.

delegation abroad urged Phizo to condemn the Accord and without delay.[92] They earnestly pleaded for his guidance, but he remained silent. It is held that this could not satisfy the NNC Leaders who were totally opposing the Accord. Therefore his silence was considered as an act of acceptance of the Accord.[93] Though Phizo condemned the Accord, it was reported that he accepted it to have been the work of the Shillong Accordists.[94]

At this time of crisis within the NNC leaders, the Government of Nagaland made an arrangement for negotiation with the Federal Government of Nagaland (in existence in the Eastern region of Nagaland] In June, 1978 at Pangsa village, the talks were held to discuss the non-implementation of the of the Shillong Accord Clause I and III. The Naga underground representatives strongly protested against the points put forward by the government of Nagaland. Yet the talks broke down. And it engendered the rift within the NNC leaders. The Muivah who returned from China "strongly opposed the leadership of Phizo and the policy of NNC."[95] Muivah proposed to change the system of Government in the form of Socialism and centralised government.

Herewith the 'ideological' differences erupted among the NNC leaders. Soon it went with tribal loyalties; Semas and most of the Tangkhuls supporting Isak and Muivah, but the Aos, Angamis, Chakesang, Konyak, Kheimnungam and Hemmi Nagas from Burma opposing the new Muivah policy.[96]

On 30 August, 1978, the Defence Council of the Naga Army imposed 'Martial law' in Sapha Camp* for six months. Muivah, Isak Swu, Vedan Mori and Pruning were arrested (House detentions), on 13 March 1979 the new "National Assembly"[97] session was held and S.S. Khaplang, a Hemi Naga of Burma was elected as the President of Federal Government. However, after the release of Isak Swu and Th. Muivah in May 1979.[98] The two leaders were able to win over S.S. Khaplang. Hence the three staged a counter coup d'etat' and those persons responsible for the imposition of 'martial law' was eliminated. The sudden dramatic raids by the three

* Sapha camp was once a headquarter of the NFG which is Eastern Nagaland (Burma).

leaders cost the lives of twenty top officers of the Naga Federal Government.[99] Ever since that episode in the NNC-Federal Camp, the top three leaders, Isak Swu, Th. Muivah and S.S. Khaplang broke away from the NNC (parent body of the Naga National Movement) and jointly formed the 'Nationalist Socialist Council of Nagaland' (NSCN). It is said that they had chosen to "fight to a finish for one's nation freedom"[100] to form NSCN. Thus it is argued that Shillong Accord of 1975 was responsible for the formation of the new group, which has created another chapter in the Naga National Movement.

D. Emergence and Split of NSCN

The NSCN was formed on 2 February 1980.[101] Their manifesto was based on the principle of Socialism for Economic solution and a spiritual outlook, 'Nagaland for Christ.'[102] Then they proclaimed the new Government of the "People Republic of Nagaland' with Isak Swu as Chairman S.S. Khaplang as Vice-Chairman and Th. Muivah as General Secretary. This new group has brought in a revival of the Naga National Movement in the form of Socialism. The main objective of the NSCN was to build up a 'Sovereign Christian Socialist State' of Nagaland' by declaring that they are "revolutionary patriots"[103] But after its formation rift developed within the NSCN in a short period of years among the top leaders. It was reported that Konyaks and Tangkhuls relation was not cordial[104] from the beginning. The schism was created between Tangkhul and Konyaks and the Eastern Nagas.[105] Keeping in mind tribalism was also one of the major factors for creation of the situation.

In the midst of the crisis, within the group, Indian Intelligence Raw (Research Analysis Wing) also played some role to split the NSCN on the tribal line.[106] It also appeared that in the name of the unity move, Chingang Konyak a pastor and Hokishe Sema the then Chief Minister of Nagaland complicated the situation by laying a trap for talks to confuse the NSCN leaders. The offer was said to be rejected but rumours widely spread out that Isak and Muivah had sold out the plan to oust Kaphlang, seize arms from Konyak national workers and surrender in India."[107] Shortly informations reached the NSCN headquarter. Soon, knowing the situation, the National Assembly Session was called to resolve the controversial reports, but the situation could not be solved. Leaders went on their own way and led to bloodshed in the NSCN camp. On 30 April, 1988, Muivah camp was attacked by the S.S. Kaphlang and Brigadier Khole Konyak group, killing about 140 men mostly the Tangkhuls, while 230 others including women and children were killed by bullets, hunger and sickness, some died at the hands of the Burmese armies.[108] But Th.Muivah with 33 others managed to escape and join up with Isak Swu.[109] It was reported that Isak Swu was away from the NSCN camp. After that incident NSCN was "vertically split into two factions"[110] one led by Isak Swu and Th. Muivah called NSCN(I-M) and the other led by S.S. Khaplang NSCN(K).

Some arguments given were mistrust, suspicion, ideological differences, disagreement among the leaders and inability to control the civil and political situation that led to split within the NSCN. Since 1991, the Government of India banned both the NSCN factions.

E. The Naga National Movement after A.Z. Phizo

The Shillong Accord of 1975 has done the major damage to the Naga National Movement. After the Accord, a faction of the NNC formed NSCN in 1978. Perhaps, remaining body of NNC was still under the A.Z. Phizo leadership till the early 1990s. However, after the death of A.Z. Phizo, the founding father of the Naga National Movement on 30, April 1990, it was once again divided into two groups NNC (Adino) and NNC (Khodao) over the issue of presidentship.

The problem was created after Miss Adino (Phizo daughter) was elected as the Prsident of NNC on 12th May 1990 by the NNC central committee in Kohima. But it was held that under the direction of Zashie Hurie* the President of Federal Government of Nagaland (FNG), she was elected. Therefore Khodao Yanthan** Senior Executive member of NNC London

---

* He authorised the NNC-Federal delegates to sign the Shillong Accord, 1975.

** Senior Member of NNC who lives in London and jointly works with A.Z. Phizo for many years for the Naga National Movement.

based strongly disapproved the decision taken by the NNC Central Committee. He particularly mentioned that it is "not a family or Tribal Affair",[111] stating the uniqueness of the Naga National Movement. It may be said that the conduct of election for the president became very controversial. Thus both Shillong Accordist and non-Accordist use the same word as 'NNC'. This has led to split of the NNC and the formation of a new group NNC led by Khodao NNC(K), but later on he joined in the NSCN (IM). One can conclude that ideology and tribal barriers separated the 'NNC'.[112] Though the Naga National Movement had been fragmented by different factions/groups, it can be said that all of them are fighting for the Nagas Sovereignty. They are divided by ideological differences, but struggling for the same cause.

REFERENCES

1. Y. Asoso, n. 2, p. 221.
2. Gordon, P. Means and Iqunn N., Means; Nagaland—The Agony of Ending a Guerrilla War, *Pacific Affairs* Vol. 39, No. 3–4, Fall and Winter, 1966–67, p. 297.
3. Y. Asoso, n. 2, p. 221.
4. B.G. Verghese, India's North-East Resurgent, Ethnicity, Insurgency, Government and Development. Konark Publishers, New Delhi, 1995, p. 88.
5. M.Ramunny, n. 9, p. 72.
6. Y. Asoso, n. 2, p. 222; see Ramunny, n. 9, p. 73.
7. N. Maxwell, n. 36, p. 6; see also Horam, n. 20, p. 81.
8. Alemchiba, n. 10, p. 186.
9. Ibid., p. 186.
10. Horam, n. 20, p. 84.
11. P. Basu, "The Naga Problem; An Overview" *Asian Studies*, 6(2), 1988, p. 33.
12. Horam, n. 20, p. 84.
13. Y. Asoso, n. 2, p. 224.
14. Ibid., p. 228.
15. Huska, n. 1, p. 8.
16. The Naga Problems—External Publicity Division, Ministry of External Affairs, Government of India, 1962, p. 6.
17. Huska, n. 1, p. 7.
18. B. Baboo, n. 20, p. 46.
19. Y. Asoso, n. 2, p. 230; see Ramunny, n. 9, p. 78.
20. Alemchiba, n. 10, p. 197
21. N. Maxwell, n. 36, p. 7.
22. George N., Patterson, n. 99, p. 333.

23. Lok Sabha Debate, Vol. XLIV, Second Series, 1–12 August, 1960.
24. U.G. Bower, n. 60, p. 51.
25. N. Maxwell, n. 36, p. 7.
26. Y. Asoso, n. 2, p. 236.
27. M. Ramunny, n. 9, p. 94.
28. Y. Asoso, n. 2, p. 237
29. N. Maxwell, n. 36, p. 7.
30. U.G. Bowell, n. 60, p. 59.
31. N. Maxwell, n. 36, p. 60.
32. U.G. Bower, n. 60, p. 51.
33. Ibid., p. 77.
34. Y. Aosos, n. 2, p. 239.
35. Horam, n. 20, p. 87.
36. Ibid., p. 88.
37. N. Maxwell, n. 36, p. 7.
38. Ibid., p. 7.
39. Y. Asoso, n. 2, p. 249.
40. Ibid., p. 249.
41. Y. Asoso, n. 1, p. 254.
42. N. Maxwell, "India: The Nagas and the North-East", Report n. 17, Revised Edition, Minority Rights Group, 1980, p. 7.
43. M. Horam, "Naga Insurgency" Cosmo Publications, Delhi, 1988, p. 106.
44. Rev. Michael Scott, "The Nagas: India's Problem—Or the World's? London, 1967, p. 16.
45. M. Alemchiba, "A Brief Historical Account of Nagaland", The Naga Institute of Culture, Kohima, Nagaland, 1970, p. 202.
46. M. Horam, n. 16, p. 106, Y. Asoso, n. 1, p. 267.
47. Rev. Michael Scott, n. 16, p. 17, U.G. Bower, "The Naga Problem" (Manuscript) 1967, p. 127.
48. See Appendix-IV Bilateral Agreement on Cease Fire. 14th August 1964.
49. Ibid.
50. M. Rammuny, "The World of Nagas", Northern Book Center, New Delhi, 1988, p. 104.
51. M. Aram, "Peace in Nagaland: Eight Years Story (1964–74)", Arnold Heinemann Publications, New Delhi, p. 52.
52. Ibid., p. 52.
53. M. Horam, n. 16, p. 111.
54. M. Aram, n. 24, pp. 32–33.
55. IWGIA Publications "Naga Nation Struggle against Genocide", Netherlands, 1986, p. 31.
56. Peace Mission Proposal, para 13, full text see appendix.
57. IWGIA, n. 28, p. 31, Gordon P. Means and Ingunn N. Means, "Nagaland—The Agony of Ending a Guerrilla War". *Pacific Affairs*. Vol. 39. No. 3, 4, Fall and Winter, (1966–67) p. 303.
58. Rev. Michael Scott, n. 17, p. 227.
59. Rev. Michael Scott, n. 17, p. 28.
60. M. Rammuny, n. 23, p. 150.
61. Gordon, P. Means Ingunn and Means, n. 30, p. 308, Also see B.G. Verghese, "India's North-East Resurgent: Ethnicity, Insurgency, Governance and Development", Konark Publishers, 1995, p. 92.

62. Ibid., p. 308, quoted, Private Letter from A.Z. Phizo, 9 February, 1967.
63. L. Wati, "Fact and Growth of Naga Nationalism (Mimeographed), 1993, p. 122, M. Horam, n. 15, p. 136.
64. M. Horam, n. 16, p. 140.
65. Ibid., pp. 140–41, L. Wati, n. 36, p. 125, Tajenyuba Ao, "British Occupation of Naga Country", Naga Literature Society, Mokokchung Nagaland, 1993, p. 292.
66. Tajenyuba Ao, n. 38, p. 293.
67. See M. Rammuny, n. 23, p. 174, Tajenyuba Ao, n. 38, p. 294.
68. M. Horam, n. 16, pp. 143–44.
69. Tajenyuba Ao, n. 38, p. 295.
70. M. Rammuny, n. 23, p. 177, L. Wati, n. 358, p. 127.
71. Ibid., p. 177, Tajenyuba Ao, n. 38, p. 295.
72. Tajenyuba Ao, n. 38, pp. 294–95.
73. M. Horam, n. 16, p. 161.
74. B. Baboo, "The Naga National Movement: An Analysis". *Third World Unity*, Vol. 15–16. March–April, 1979, p. 47.
75. IWGIA, n. 28, p. 32.
76. M. Rammuny, n. 23, pp. 192–93.
77. IWGIA, n. 28, pp. 32–33, B.G. Verghese, n. 34, p. 94.
78. M. Rammuny, n. 23, p. 196, L. Wati, n. 36, p. 126.
79. L. Wati, n. 36, p. 126.
80. M. Rammuny, n. 23, p. 197.
81. Tajenyuba Ao, n. 38, pp. 195–96, L. Wati, n. 36, p. 126, M. Rammuny, n. 23, p. 197.
82. Tajenyuba Ao, n. 38, p. 297.
83. L. Wati, n. 36, p. 141.
84. See appendix VI of Shillong Accord.
85. M. Rammuny, n. 23, p. 226, L. Wati, n. 36, p. 142.
86. L. Wati, n. 36, p. 142.
87. M. Rammuny, n. 23, p. 227.
88. M. Horam, n. 16, p. 186.
89. See appendix VII—Phizo-Desai talks in London, 1997.
90. B.G. Verghese, n. 34, p. 95.
91. NSCN Publication, "A Brief Political Account of Nagaland" (Unpublished), 1993, p. 31.
92. Ibid., p. 131
93. Tajenyuba Ao, n. 38, p. 299.
94. M. Horam, n. 16, p. 188.
95. P. Pashen Khiamnungan, "Partition in Eastern Nagaland", *Nagaland Post*, 3 January, 1997.
96. L. Wati, n. 36, p. 164.
97. Ibid., p. 169.
98. P. Pashem Khiamnungan, n. 68, 3 January, 1972.
99. L. Wati, n. 36, pp. 164–65; Tajenyuba Ao, n. 38, p. 301.
100. Tajenyuba Ao, n. 38, p. 301.
101. L. Wati, n. 36, p. 165.
102. Tajenyuba Ao, n. 38, pp. 301–302.
103. Ibid., p. 301.
104. Tajenyuba Ao, n. 38, p. 304.

105. Tongmeth, D. Nekong, "Split of NSCN", *Nagaland Post*, 2 December, 1996.
106. Ibid., Tongmeth, D. Nekong.
107. B.G. Verghese, n. 34, p. 95.
108. Ibid., p. 95.
109. Ibid., pp. 95–6.
110. Tajenyuba Ao, n. 38, p. 304.
111. L. Wati, n. 35, p. 170.
112. B.G. Verghese, n. 34, p. 101.

CHAPTER FIVE

The Naga National Movement: International Perspectives

Most problems have grown beyond the control of individual nation-states and the Indo-Naga problem is no exception. The degree of international influence depends on the institutions and social and political arrangement inside countries, eg. India, Myanmar (Burma) and China. The asymmetrical relationship with New Delhi with blunders and missed opportunities on both sides frustrated and disillusioned the Naga leadership which turned to "internationalising" the movement. International society is emphasised in theory at least the values of restraint and rejection of war and violence but it can also facilitate the formation of misconceptions. It does not always produce the best possible definition of a conflict-situation. The hope of an ideological and strategic inventory with the help of China for example, proved to be idealistic since what was at issue did not affect the core interests of that country. Moreover cultural pre-disposition are not always expressed with patience and farsightedness. If the Indians have been heavy handed in dealing with ethno-nationalism, the Chinese traditionally look upon Vietnamese as the southern savages and are no more open and tolerant to the Nagas. The Nagas have learnt that internationalisation operates differentially and without cognitive consistency.

A. Bifurcation of the Naga Hills

The Nagas living in both countries of India and Burma inhabited the most vital areas of India, Burma (Myanmar) and China for centuries. This 'Buffer Zone' is equally important to all the neighbouring countries for strategic reasons. Before the advent of the British, the Nagas lived on a contiguous region without any national or international demarcation, although the various Naga tribes were never under one administrative rule.

Ever since the British conquest of Assam by the treaty of Yandaboo in 1826 with the Burmese king, the India-Burma boundary demarcation was drawn unilaterally by the British 'imperialist for their administrative convenience'. Thus boundary line passed through the present states of Nagaland, Manipur and Mizo hills in Indian side, and the Kachin states, Naga hills and Chin hills on the Burmese sides.[1] Thus one sided boundary line which divided the Nagas into many has further magnified the Naga problems.

Since the British occupation of some parts of Naga hills, the question arises, as to how the British India Government unilaterally divided the Naga's inhabited hills into Assam, Manipur and Burma. Perhaps the intention of the boundary demarcation was to divide the Nagas in order to thwart from any revolt against the imperial rule. Though the Nagas were disunited and too weak to protest against the mighty British, the Nagas realised that the British departure from the Indian sub-continent was imminent. And they (Nagas) prepared a comprehensive memorandum and submitted to the Simon Commission which visited Kohima in 1929, saying that "leave us alone to determine for ourselves as in ancient times."[2] Memorandum stated that Nagas do not want to live by any alien domination either by India or Burma. But the Nagas' demand was not acceptable to the British Government.

However in 1937, Burma was finally separated from the Indian sub-continent,[3] and India got its independence in 1947 from the British. However, India-Burma boundary which runs through the Naga hills in India and Burma became a outstanding problem for both the countries. The boundary line that was drawn by the British administrator was little known to Nagas who were living in that border areas for centuries. In defiance to the British handing over the Nagas to India and Burma the Naga National movement was launched from 1946 for the Nagas independent. This engendered the Naga unification movement through out the Naga Inhabited Areas.

To settle India-Burma boundary problem the Prime Minister of India Jawaharlal Nehru and the Premier of Burma U. Nu jointly visited Kohima, Imphal and the Tuensang Frontier areas in 1953.[4] But the two Prime Ministers were unable to resolve the boundary disputes of the legacy of British India Government. Indeed, the Nagas revolted from this frontier areas bordering Burma for the Nagas Independent. This resulted into the Indo-Naga Armed Conflict in 1955. Further, the Frontier areas became a major strategic location for the Nagas. Henceforth, the Naga's underground used these border areas as a free passage for arms aid and military training. Here, they established their main military base with the help of the Eastern Nagas of Burma. Subsequently, this enabled the Nagas to contact with the Burmese insurgents of Kachin, Karen, and Shans who were simultaneously fighting against the union of Burma for their independence.[5]

Till 1960's, the Burmese Government did not intercept the Naga insurgent of using their territory.[6] However, the situation changed abruptly in the border areas after the suspension of U Nu Government by the Revolutionary Military Junta General Nee Win in 1962.[7] This change in leadership in Burma had made a big riddle to the Naga insurgents. The Burmese Government restricted the Nagas of using their territory as passage to East Pakistan for arms and military training.

Further the strengthening of Indo-Burmese relationship consequently led to the resolution of the two countries who concluded to resolve and to prevent the Nagas of trekking to east Pakistan and China.[8]

Despite the strategy, the question of boundary demarcation became a grave concern for both the countries. The Nagas by now had already made an alliance with the same ethnic Mongoloid stocks of Chins, Karens, Kachins and Arkansas and succeeded to link with Peking.[9] This posed a serious threat to Indian security.

Hence, in order to find a permanent settlement of the boundary problem, India-Burma boundary agreement was signed on 10th March 1967 by colonel Kyi Maung on behalf of the Government of Burma and K.M. Kannampilly of the Indian Government.[10] This agreement resolved to "delineate, delimit and demarcate the boundary of 909 sq. miles between the two countries."

It has been argued that the International boundary line was drawn arbitrarily without the consent of the Nagas. By this agreement, the Naga hills was demarcated officially and the people were divided to live in the two countries. From the geographical factors, it shows that the contiguous Naga territory (Hills) was split into two regions of South Asia and the South East Asia. Consequently, today there are 40 odd Naga tribes, out of which six Naga tribes are found in Burma, i.e. the Konyak Nagas, the Hemie Nagas, the Pangmei Nagas, the Puchury Nagas, the Tangkhul Nagas and the Khiemnungan Nagas, and the rest are in India. "In Longwa and 16 other villages in Mon District (Nagaland state) Longkhao village in Tirap district (Arunachal state) and Tusaw village in Ukhrul district (Manipur) half of the village lands are in Burma and the other half in India. In fact, in Longwa village so called International Boundary between India and Burma actually splits the Angh's (Village Chief) house into half."[11] To show how arbitrarily the International boundary line was made.

At present some of the Naga tribes like Konyak Nagas are found in Mon district in Nagaland and in Burma, the Pochury Nagas are also in Nagaland and in Burma; the Tangkhul Nagas are both in Manipur and in Somra tract in Burma;[12] "the Khiamnungan Nagas who have 23 villages within Nagaland States but 137 villages are in Burma."[13]

Here the question arises as to whether the Naga political problem is really a domestic one or it has international dimension. The argument is that the Naga political issue is not confined to India alone, but it goes across the International border. It implicates two countries, politically as well as geographically, which clearly indicates that the Naga National Movement has become International problem/issue. This international boundary was outrightly rejected by the Nagas. Though the Nagas are scattered over in two countries, the Naga liberation movement is intensified to integrate all the Naga inhabited areas of both India and Burma.

The Naga struggle for independence has to bring all the Nagas-inhabited areas of India and Burma together and to form a separate country which is called 'Greater Nagaland'.

Here the Notional Map of Naga Domain shows all the contiguous Naga territories in India and Burma indicating the various Naga tribes split and living in two countries demarcated by arbitrary international boundary.

The Notional Map of the Naga Domain

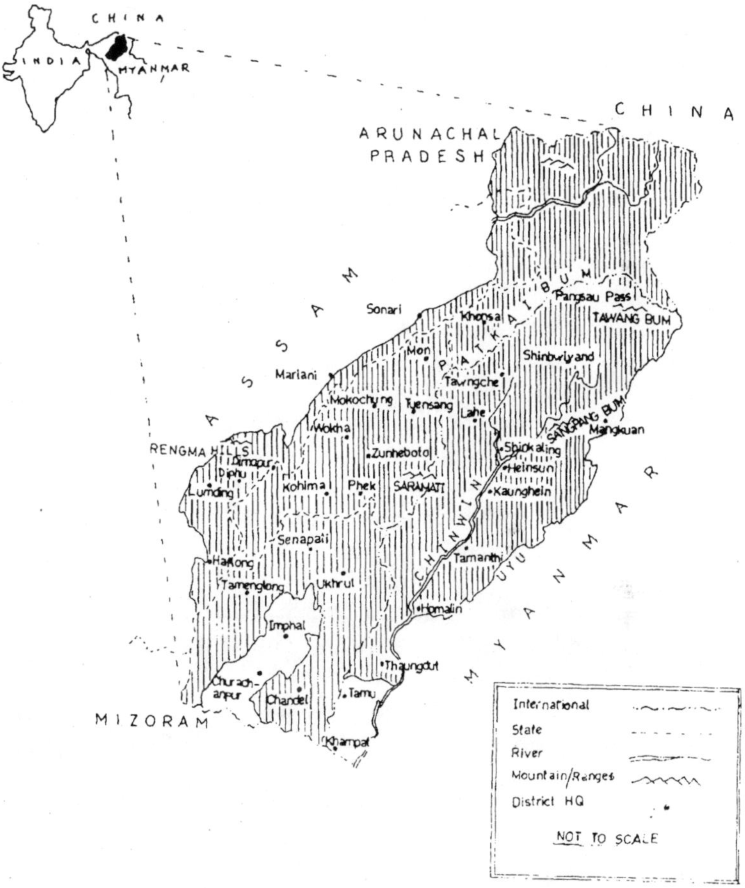

Source: Naga Student Federation (NSF) 1995
Naga National Council (NNC) (unpublished)
Naga Reserach Scholars

B. External Linkages

i) Naga Relations with Pakistan

General Mowu, the first Naga underground sought sponsorship and to represent the Naga case to the UN. On 15 October 1956, met Ata-Ur Rahman, the Chief Minister of East Pakistan, who refused the request which was said to be against the International Law.[14] The Naga-Pakistan contact was made possible through the Pakistan agent, running an Assistant High Commission office at Shillong (Meghalaya) in the middle of 1950s. Eventually the government of India asked them to wind up their office when it came to light the Pakistan's cohesion with the Naga underground. But by that time the Nagas had already established their base in Dacca (capital of Bangladesh).

In December 1956, A.Z. Phizo the President of NNC stepped out to East Pakistan (Bangladesh) to deliberately internationalise the Naga issue and seek foreign support for the Nagas. Initially Pakistan did not want to get involved in India directly. They "suggested A.Z. Phizo to go to London to raise the Naga issue in the UN" But at the same time they promised to give "moral support, military aid, supply of arms and ammunition and training facilities."[15] Then from Dacca, Phizo went to Karachi (capital of Pakistan) and finally landed in London on 12 June, 1960 via Zurich. From London he conducted anti Indian propaganda on the activities of Indian armies in Nagaland. At the behest of Phizo in the early part of 1957, the Naga underground went to East Pakistan through the dark forest of Burmese territory and established their main base in Dacca. With Pakistani's support they opened military training centre for the Naga underground such as "Rangamati Ruma, Bandarbati, Rangkhis forest area, Alikadam and other places in Chitagong Hill tracts."[16] Since then the Nagas succeeded in their travel through East Pakistan for military arms and training. Between 1959 to 1965 as many as four batches of Naga Federal Army went to East Pakistan. In 1963, the first batch of 173 trained Naga army returned to Nagaland from East Pakistan and brought along with them 12 two-inch mortars, 16 height machine guns, 30 stein-guns, 20 pistols, 100 rifles, 190 hand grenades and 74 steins grenades and other ammunition and explosive."[17] While crossing the International border some were captured by the Indian armies with documents, which revealed that "the Pakistan Government are helping the Naga guerrillas with money and arms."[18]

The second batch of 202 returned to Nagaland with huge arms of 87 mm mortars, two medium machine guns, two pistols, 68 automatic rifles, 400 hand grenades and about 300 rounds of ammunitions. Then the third batch of about 150 men also returned in June 1964, bringing 14 light machine guns, 40 stein guns, 80 rifles, 5 pistols, 300 hand grenades and about 200 rounds of ammunitions per weapon.[19] Those arms were used by the Nagas to fight against the Indian armies. At the time Pakistan trainee officers exhorted the Naga army to "fight without losing heart" till the Nagas attained Independence, "if the Nagas continued to fight, Pakistan would support them."[20] But the liberation of East Pakistan was a deadly blow for the Nagas. During the Indo-Pakistan war of 1971, four Nagas underground leaders* along with some Pakistan troops surrendered to the Indian forces in Dacca on 22 December 1971.

By early 1960s the Naga underground was able to penetrate into Burma and made good contact with the Burmese insurgents in upper Burma. This was achieved through the help of the Eastern Naga Revolution Council (ENRC) of the Nagas based in Burma who were also fighting the Burmese. After the formation of the NNC, both the Naga insurgents of India and Burma shared the common interest for forming 'Greater Nagaland', integrating all the Naga inhabited areas on either side of the Indo-Burmese border. Though the Nagas are divided, living in two countries, they have physical and social affinities. In fact, some Burmese Nagas also speak dialects which were spoken by the Nagas from India. Such as the ...Konyaks and Kiamnungangs.[21] The Burmese Naga hills is one place where many Naga insurgents from the Indian sides are given help and shelter.

---

* General Thinosellie, his deputy Brigadier, Nidelio and two other brigadiers were surrendered in Dacca.

At one time infact the Naga Federal Government and the Kachin* Independence Army (KIA) (which were also fighting against the Burmese Government) signed an agreement to hold joint operation on both sides of the Indo-Burma border. It was also reported that rebels of Burma, Bangladesh and India were supposed to go for a 'Unified Command' in the later part of 1974. Comprising Mizo's (MNF) Nagas (NFG) Chakma Liberation Front and the Shanti Bahni (of the Chittagong Hill Tract of Bangladesh),[22] Eastern Nagas of (Burma).[23] Consequently in contact with the Burmese Insurgents, the Naga underground found a comfortable corridor sanctuary as rest camp and sympathiser all the way to China.

ii) Naga Connection with China

The Naga Insurgents had established contact with China since the Indo-China war of 1962. It was through the Pakistani influence that Naga insurgents sought help from Peking for the liberation of Nagaland. That was a time when India and China were almost on the edge of war on boundary issue. Then the Nagas Federal Government Prime Minister Kukhato Sema wrote to Chinese Prime Minister Chou En-Lai saying that "Nagas would give full support, if China attacked India through Nagaland," but this did not happen. Interestingly, they attacked from Arunachal Padesh (NEFA). But the Naga guerrillas who were fighting against India did not even lift a finger to help the Chinese army.[24] Instead, the NNC President A.Z. Phizo who gave a press conference in London on 15 November 1962 offered the Indian Government 40,000 Nagas Federal armies to fight against the Chinese, if India agreed to grant the Naga demand of Independence.[25] One might say that Phizo did not want the help from the Communist Countries. As on religious ground he might lose the public support if he ties up with the Chinese, against the wishes of the Nagas most of whom are Christians. Earlier there was no substantial tie with the Chinese. But in order to achieve the Nagas Independence Phizo turned to China. However, after the Chinese aggression of India in 1962, General Kaito Sema flew

* The Kachin territory which lies in the North-East of Burma bordering the Yunan province of China.

to Peking from London as the envoy of Phizo, and Peking unrolled its 'red carpet' for him. Since then Peking had started rendering help to the Nagas.[26] It is evident that "the Chinese are having close link and attention to the ethnic and linguistic groups of their frontier areas with both India and Burma."[27] It is possible that if Peking had not helped the Nagas underground, the Naga leaders might have played a different role.[28]

After the Chinese Government had given assurance to the Nagas for their support, they invited young educated Nagas for training in arms and ammunition. It became a morale booster for the Naga Federal Government. But also understandably the Church and state government became vehemently hostile about the movement of the underground Nagas.

Hence, the first batch of Naga army led by Brigadier Thinosellie and Th. Muivah went to China in 1966, with about 300 Naga federal army through northern Burma. They successfully crossed the International border under the guidance and assistance from the Eastern Nagas, Kachins, Shans and Karens and went to the southern Chinese province of Yunan for military and political aid to fight against the Indians. Brigadier Thenosillie and Th. Muivah was designated as 'Ambassador plenipotentiary' of the Naga Federal Government (NFG).[29] It was reported that they stayed there for two years and established the diplomatic ties and made arrangements for the Nagas Federal Government. Thereafter, they returned from China with huge arms and ammunitions. But after reaching Nagaland they were attacked by Indian Security forces in Jotsoma near Kohima. Twenty five Nagas guerrillas were captured along with Chinese arms such as, 60mm mortars, 7.62 SKS carbine, AK 47 automatic rifles, US made carbines, Medium machine guns and quantities of medical supplies and clinical equipment's used in military operations. Some documents and diaries were seized containing the Mao Tse-Tung famous principles of guerrilla's war:

> [We are the advocates of abolition of war, we do not want war, but war can only be abolished through war and in order to get rid of the gun, it is necessary to take up guns." Political power comes out from the barrel of guns. (*Mao's Little Red Book*, p. 74)].

Then in their diary entry about the Mao's tactics of guerrilla warfare:

> The enemy advances, we retreat, the enemy camps, we harass, the enemy tires, we attack, the enemy retreats, we pursue.[30]

It became a good inspiration and moral booster to the Naga guerrillas. Another note, book and diary also indicated the Chinese Government suggestions to the Nagas to form a government in exile. It specified that, (1) The Government in exile would be based at a suitable point in Chinese territory contiguous to the Indian border. (2) The Chinese would openly support the Nagas cause on the pattern of their support to the Government in exile, and (3) The Chinese would guide the foreign relations of the Government in exile.[31] But the Nagas connection with the Chinese was not favoured by some sections of the Naga Federal Government and also the Church were suspicious about the Communist China. This had created division within the Nagas.

Th. Muivah who was then Ambassador plenipotentiary of the Naga Federal Government to China was taken by the Chinese hosts to Hanoi (North Vietnam) to see the theatre of war, how the Vietnamese had fought against the Americans 'imperialist'. Shortly some batches of Naga armies were sent to Hanoi from China "for intensive guerrilla" training, "where they could practice guerrilla tactics against modern weaponary".[32] It became an 'open secret' of Chinese helping the Nagas with arms and military training and sent it back to Nagaland to fight against the Indian government. Once the Taiwan Foreign Minister, De Wei Tao-Ming in the UN Assembly on 22 October, 1969 accused the Chinese Government of giving military training to the Naga guerrillas in the Yunan province to fight against the Indian armies.[33] At once there was a talk between Mrs. Gandhi, Prime Minister of India and General Ne Win Chairman of the Burmese Revolutionary Council on 16–22 March, 1968 in New Delhi to prevent the Nagas underground track to China.[34] It was equally important for both the countries to curb the Naga underground movements but they could not seal the border. However, when, it came to the notice that the Chinese were giving help to the Nagas underground, the Government of India took a serious view and strongly protested against the Chinese Government of interference in India's 'internal affairs'. They warned the Chinese Government that they would be entirely responsible for the consequences.[35] The Chinese have been assuring New Delhi that they have stopped all aid to the Nagas. Perhaps, the Chinese called the rebel Nagas and Mizos as 'Nationalist' who were waging war against the 'reactionary Indian troops and police' for their 'National Liberation'."[36] Moreover they also encouraged the Nagas, Mizos and the Burmese insurgents to form a 'Federal State' including Chittagong Hill tract of Bangladesh. For that purpose they opened the military training camps in Yunan province and Burma.[37] In fact, from time to time small batches of Chinese trained Naga guerrillas returned to Nagaland.

In the wider context of International rivalries in South-East Asia, China, is one of the potential country and capable of giving threat to their immediate neighbour. China sees the Naga Areas as quite important to India's security defence. Therefore it is in their interest and policy to support the Naga insurgents and threaten India. Knowingly, if the Naga Independence Movement continued it would create the instability and unrest in India for their advantage.

iii) Naga-CIA Connection

In the late 1960s the American CIA had extended their activities by supporting financially to the Naga Movement. This was testified by John Smith a Secret Agent of the US.[38] He also admitted that American spies "handed the tribal leaders several millions rupees, weapons and secret instruction prepared in Washington"[39] In this context, to supervise the North-East India they came out with the research project called 'Project Brahmaputra'. The US International Communication Agency issued a circular on 21 June 1979 entitled 'Project Brahmaputra' to conduct research in the North-Eastern state, including Sikkim and Bhutan. According to the scope of the project, the research teams would "conduct public opinion poll on the constitutional position in different North-Eastern

State and find out the possibility of forming a New State."[40]

It is a well known fact that not only Pakistan and China helping the Nagas underground but the CIA also has been operating in the North-East since late 1950s through the Indian employees and their agents too. Till 1971, the US continued to be the patron of the insurgents. But when the Naga underground moved closer to Peking, their activities shifted to Bangkok.

From the middle of 1970's the new radical group dominated the Naga National Movement. After the Shillong Accord of 1975, (between the government of India and the Nagas underground representatives) the Naga National Movement led by NNC was fragmented. Further, this had led to the emergence of new group called the National Socialist Council of Nagaland (NSCN) in 1978. It may be said that the term 'Socialist' was inherited from the Communist China after the establishment of connection with Peking. Once again, this group revived the Naga movement with implication for International Politics. But this new nationalist group also split in 1980, between NSCN (IM) and NSCN (K) . However, the two groups are operating from the different International arena. NSCN (K) is successfully operating from Myanmar (Burma). But the other group NSCN (IM) which came out to be the strongest amongst the Nagas underground groups, are operating successfully from Thailand (Bangkok).

iv) Nagas and United Nations

Since A.Z. Phizo, the President of NNC tried to internationalise the Naga issue through some agencies, he also attempted to raise the Naga issue at the UN. To highlight the Naga political problems, he conducted an anti-Indian propaganda in London, and his presence there was widely publicised by the London observer, from the middle of 1960s.

The London based Minority Rights Groups, Neville Maxwell, brought out a booklet entitled 'India and the Nagas' accusing India with a series of atrocities, following the end of the cease-fire agreement in 1972.[41] Again, Patrick Montgomery Secretary to the Anti-Slavery Society, compared the India's pacification drive and alleged atrocities committed in

Nagaland to Mozambique, and urged the British people to speak up for the Nagas as the later supported the British allied forces during the World War II.[42] At once Phizo submitted a petition to the International Commission of Jurist, which charged "India's as carrying out genocide against the sheer minority Nagas."[43]

He tried to take up the Naga case in UN through Pakistan and China. In May 1964, Z.A. Bhutto, Foreign Minister of Pakistan, stated in the UN Secretary Council that the Indian representative had been silent about "systematic and brutal persecution of the Nagas, which has been going on in Eastern India for many years."[44] But there was no response from the other members, they still considered it would be interference in the Indian 'domestic affairs.' In November 1965, Reverend Michael Scott wrote to the Secretary General of the UN, asking him to take up the Naga case. Again in October 1966, he tried to open up the Naga question before the UN in the meeting of the Fourth Committee on Colonialism,* but did not succeed.[45]

From the beginning of the Naga National movement, Nagas were hoping support from the British and the Americans, for the Liberation of Nagaland. It was with such expectation that A.Z. Phizo also chose London instead of the other countries to raise the Naga issue in the UN through their support. After Phizo landed up in London on 4, April 1967, he went to US seeking their support and to put up the Naga issues through American lobbies. It was reported that he once stated the Naga issue in the New York Times on 27, April 1967. But his visit raised a mild controversy between the U.S. and the Indian Government. The Government of India took objection to his visit stating that the U.S. Government was giving platform to Phizo to highlight the Naga issue. The U.S. Government responded to the Indian Government that Phizo came only for medical treatment for his partial facial paralyses.[46] Because of the Indian Government resentment, the U.S. did not allow him to lobby for the Naga case in the UN.

---

* Scott represented as a petitioner on the question of South-East Africa, indirectly to raise Naga question and it was supported by the Pakistan delegates, but strongly protested by the Indian delegates Bhagwat Jha Azad , the case was noted but not discussed.

v) Naga and International Fora

It is true that the Naga rebels are working hand in hand with all the insurgent groups in both India and Burma. Further the NSCN (IM) became more exposed among the other Naga underground groups and successfully expanded their operation in the global arena. For the first time in the history of the Naga movement, NSCN (IM) had successfully brought more sophisticated arms from the neighbouring countries crossing the Indian arena. Significantly, this operation was code named *'Operation Red Sea'* followed by the *'Operation Jordan'*.[47] This had given a moral boost to the Nagas. On 23 January, 1993 the Naga political movement received a shot in arm by achieving the admission of Nagaland into the membership of the Unrepresentative Nations Peoples Organisation (UNPO),[48] with its headquarter at Hague. The Naga movement leaders such as Isak and Muivah NSCN (IM) have successfully addressed the Naga case to the United Nations Committee for Indigenous People and Human Rights.[49] The UN Committee has accepted the rights of Nagas for self–determination. Subsequently, some offices of the Naga political movement have already been opened in several countries i.e. Bangkok, Geneva, New York and Manila. Presently, the Naga cases are sponsored by the Flemish, Swiss and Belgians.[50] This boosted the morals among the Nagas adding, much needed support for the Naga case.

It may be said that Nagas joining the international forum is a two-pronged strategy. It can act against the Government of India, i.e. by highlighting the Human Right abuse against the Nagas. In this process Nagas had been able to garner support of the Amnesty International and 'Naga Vigil group',* to highlight and lobby the cause of the Nagas in various international forums. Secondly, it can be said that the cold war politics in the international system was favourable during the 60s to get external support for the Nagas, example, Pakistan, China and Intelligence Agencies of the United States (CIA). This external support brought the Naga National Movement into new international dimensions.

---

* Naga Vigil which has based in London.

Moreover Naga movement have an 'irredentism' claim over the Naga inhabited area of Myanmar (Burma) as independent states (Eastern Nagas). It has necessarily involved Burma too. Although it may be instrumental in furthering the cause of the Nagas so far as the part of Naga hills, this has undoubtedly implicated both India and Burma in the international context.

The ideological, political and military tensions between the three states have ensured that the ethno-political situation remains precarious. Regardless of the actual degree of national consciousness of the Nagas they have found themselves mired in intractable disputes where they have been accused of separatism and anti-national activities. The orientation towards "coercive regional primacy" has played a significant role in creating adversarial approaches. If a needs based integrative approach were developed and aspects of interdependence were emphasised over those of competition, diminished conflict probabilities would emerge.

C. Relinquishment of Regional Hegemony Aspirations

The implication is that the Nagas are not necessarily seeking a solution through internationalisation. The failure on the part of the Government of India to make a demonstration of intent led repeatedly to the failure of negotiations and to the rejection of political compromise. With the advantage of insight we can see that there were several stages of Naga struggle. Strategies of "state-contraction" could have been evolved to suite different configuration of Naga cultural dispositions. Instead the pursuit of hegemonic conception by the Indian ruling class and the absence of any way to interpret the long term cumulative processes of Naga society resulted in sudden and drastic transformation into civil war and collapse of civil society. Real progress can be made in the stabilisation of the Naga area's political future by maintaining a clear distinction between civil and military security and working towards comprehensive security between India, Myanmar and China. The Nagas have experienced an ebb and flow with respect to internationally backed insurgency. The more moderate version of the right of self-determination leaves considerable room for widely disparate interpretations bearing on revolutionary doctrine and fraternal help from abroad. The striking feature of recent Naga revolutionary practice is to avoid doctrinal efforts to consummate new arrangements for autonomy.

D. Functional Sovereignty as a Viable means of Self-determination

The Naga experience with "international politics" has led to a unique ideological position, which can be described as theoretical eclecticism. Different variables relating to India, China, Myanmar, United States and other Western countries have effected the emerging relationship between (a) systemic, (b) domestic and (c) cognitive forces operating as the organising principles for the Nagas elite. The drawing of lessons have shaped elite beliefs and are forcing decision makers towards pragmatism and more moderate and self-limiting behaviour.

Naga leaders increasingly base their decision on "functional sovereignty" as a result of paradigm shift which perceives science, technology and communication as necessitating basic changes in the ongoing Naga struggle for fulfilment of their "manifest destiny". Although the Indian body politics has not kept pace with these shifts in Naga perceptions the possibility of creating a new multi-centred network should have an influence on the issue of self-determination and constitutional change. There is a continuum extending from political militants to moderates who are now committed to peace building based upon institutional reform, fair elections, international monitoring, and political rehabilitation through functional sovereignty and flexible political strategies. Recent peace keeping experience in South Africa and Northern Ireland have suggested questions like the following as a means to live up to the expectations of the international community:

> What are the resources available to the Nagas for mutual co-operation and how far this has been optimised?
>
> In what sense can the Nagas develop an appropriate degree of self-determination to suit their indigenous culture?
>
> What are the financial and technological resources for the Nagas in order to end their economic exploitation and political subordination?

What are the preconditions for traditional transactions that would contribute to peace and prosperity of the Nagas and not merely express dissatisfaction with the existing system?

What initiatives towards self-governance and greater autonomy will simultaneously bring peace to Naga communities and facilities devolution of power?

E. The Domain of Ambiguity in Defusing Present Tensions

There is a growing feeling among Indian elite that important policy options for the Naga problem have been effectively removed from the political agenda by obsolete strategic conceptions. A new set of elite beliefs in New Delhi is leading to radical reappraisal of threat perceptions in the Northeast in general and with regard to the Naga people in particular. It is increasingly realised that articulation of underlying threats, traumas and aspirations of the parties engaged in protracted conflict is essential so that the analysis of conflict can move towards integrative explorations of underlying needs and values. The international setting also encourages reframing of underlying Naga problems and designing solutions. Instead of thrusting Indian constitutional norms, Indian elite opinion is veering round to the view that "political and legal fuzziness" is of value in reaching compromises acceptable to both sides. What Sir John Thomas has referred to as the "domain of ambiguity" can sometimes help to transform violence, anarchy and chaos: politically stabilising arrangements, leaving awkward questions of sovereignty to be worked out later on with flexibility.

REFERENCES

1. Y. Asoso, "The Rising Naga", Vivek Publishing House, New Delhi, 1979, p. 327.
2. Indian Commission on 26 March, 1928./10-1-1929.
3. Y. Asoso, n. 1, p. 327.
4. Y. Asoso, n. 1, p. 329.
5. Ibid., n. 1, p. 329.
6. Ibid., n. 1, p. 329.
7. Ibid., n. 1, p. 329.

8. Ibid., n. 1, p. 330.
9. Ibid., n. 1, p. 330.
10. Ibid., n. 1, pp. 330–331.
11. NSF. Seminar Paper, "The Naga Problem: An Account", New Delhi, 14 December, 1995, p. 1.
12. Ibid., n. 12, p. 1.
13. Nirmal Nibedon, "North-East India: The Ethnic Explosion, Lancers Publishers, New Delhi, 1981. p. 187.
14. Y. Asoso, n. 1, pp. 301–02.
15. Ibid., p. 303.
16. Ibid., p. 303
17. M. Horam, n. 16, p. 94.
18. Ibid., p. 97.
19. Ibid., p. 98.
20. Ibid., n. 16, p. 97.
21. Ibid., p. 103.
22. M. Horam, n. 16, p. 101.
23. Ibid., p. 101.
24. M. Horam, n. 16, p. 94.
25. Y. Asoso, n. 1, pp. 343–44, quoted from the New York Times, 16 November, 1962.
26. V.K. Sarin, "India's North-East in Flames", Vikas Publishing House, Ltd., New Delhi, 1982, p. 17.
27. M. Horam, n. 16, p. 105.
28. V.K. Sarin, n. 99, p. 12.
29. Y. Asoso, n. 1, p. 346.
30. Y. Asoso, n. 1, p. 351; M. Horam, n. 16, p. 144; Gundevia, "War and Peace in Nagaland", Palit and Palit Publishers, New Delhi, 1975, p. 194.
31. M. Horam, n. 16, pp. 145.
32. N. Maxwell, n. 15, p. 13.
33. M. Horam, n. 16, p. 146.
34. Y. Asoso, n. 1, p. 349.
35. Ibid., p. 354.
36. Ibid., 359, quoted from Peking Radio Report, 9 July and 27 September, 1970.
37. Ibid., p. 361.
38. V.I.K. Sarin, n. 99, p. 23.
39. Ibid., n. 99, p. 23.
40. Ibid., p. 23.
41. Y. Asoso, n. 1, p. 311.
42. Ibid., p. 311, quoted from The Times, London, 14 November, 1973.
43. Y. Asoso, n. 1, p. 323.
44. Ibid., p. 323, quoted, The Myth of Independence, London, 1969, p. 180.
45. Y. Asoso, n. 1, pp. 323–24.
46. Ibid., n. 1, p. 317.
47. Tajenyuba Ao, n. 38, p. 306.
48. Ibid., p. 306.
49. See appendix, Isak Swu Speech at Geneva UN Conference on Indigenous Peoples 1993.
50. Tajenyuba Ao, n. 37, p. 307.

CHAPTER SIX

Conclusion

The Naga ethnic movement initiated a peaceful process which was conceived in terms of 'flexible and graduated forms of self determination'. If the Nagas had not been denied the legitimate expression of their community identities and tribal aspirations, they would have pursued their aims through peaceful means. In making these claims we are echoing arguments which emerge when issue areas are defined objectively. One of the most difficult problems of judging and evaluating information on the Naga ethnic movement is that subsequent armed resistance has created a circle of cause and effect in which a generalised state of war has been asserted as the norm. Then Naga ethnic movement was focussed on self-help to secure honourable existence for the Nagas and indeed it had the predisposition for a long-term accommodation with the Indian State.

The initial impetus of the principle of Naga self determination was induced by de-colonization by the British, and the aims were pursued with considerable flexibility and an orderly transition to Naga independence could have been secured.

The study aims at developing expertise in map making on Indo-Naga issues so that tools of conflict resolution and peace building can be effectively employed. It suggests that the hegemonic strategy by India has not been helpful on the Naga side. The study sees an opportunity for leaders who are committed to peace and stability but also understand the sources of power in Naga society and can control the continuing strategic element in the process of negotiation. There is need also to constantly stretch the Naga intellectual horizon for understanding the different tracts of international and national progress towards peace, and also tackle the more fundamental social class inequalities prevailing in Naga societies. The Naga movements should articulate the need to monitor violation of human rights by the states and the militant groups. Since such a violations are no longer tolerated by the world community.

In the context of the Nagas, their early societies have characterized by practice of head-hunting between and within the tribes. The Nagas were neither in a position to be united nor did they reach or felt the need to organise themselves under one banner. They remained untouched and cut off from the higher civilization.

But the advent of the British and their administrative system has created the sense of ethnic consciousness and separate identity amongst the Nagas. They felt themselves to be bound together by common ties of race, history and culture. Thus ethnic consciousness is a dynamic factors of the growth of Naga Nationalism.

Interestingly, during the British colonial rule in India, they hardly attempted to conquer and control over the Naga hills. From 1879 to 1945 they could not make any agreement with the Nagas as their subject. They occupied only some parts of Naga Hills for their administrative convenience, loosely administered and treated separately the Nagas as a different ethnic stock with the plain people. This feeling of ethnic identity or consciousness of their being different from others was largely responsible for the Naga National Movement. Also at the same time on the eve of First and Second World War the Nagas got opportunities to come in contact with the civilized countries. The experiences gained from the war, while fighting for their national pride, enlightened the spirit of the Nagas to strengthen their oneness and also emphasized the differences with the rest of India. This has contributed to the Nagas struggle for the independence.

The post independent India is marked by the beginning of the Naga's National Movement. The Naga problem surfaced with the withdrawal of the British India Government.

At the time of the British departure, the Naga National Council (NNC) requested for an Interim Government for a specific period of ten years. However, the British India Government refused to interfere in the matter and left the fate of the Nagas in a situation of uncertainty. This has created a vacuum between the Nagas and the Government of India.

In such situation, in an attempt to decide the future of the Nagas, the 9-Point Hydari Agreement was signed in June 1947 between NNC and the Government of India. But the agreement failed to meet the Nagas aspirations. In clause 9 of the agreement, both the parties adopted opposing views to decide the future of the Nagas after the ten years. Whatever the controversy it involves an interpretation of that particular clauses, and therefore this part of the agreement has not been implemented by the then Nehru Government. It may be said that this has been the turning point in the Naga problem. Had the Government been implemented the agreement, it would have resulted in some concrete outcome shape towards the solution of the Nagas problem. But this opportunity was missed out. Instead it resulted into complication of the issue and widened the gap between the Nagas and the Government of India.

Later on the Naga Hill was included under Sixth Schedule of the Indian Constitution, without any consultation with the Nagas. But this was considered by the NNC as betrayal of the Nagas by the Government. It is argued that this was contrary to or inconsistent with the 9-Point Hydari Agreement. Resentment to the above arrangement the NNC under the aegis of A.Z. Phizo conducted 'plebiscite' on 16 March 1957 throughout the Naga Hills to decide the fate of the Nagas, as to whether to remain within Indian domination or to go for Nagas Independence. Results showed that 99.9% of the Nagas opted for an independent state.

However the Government of India could not accept this plebiscite results. Instead they viewed that some extremist Nagas were asking for Independence. Indeed, the results of the plebiscite which was tabulated on 16 May 1952 was seen by the Nagas as a people's mandate. Even Eastern Nagas (Burma) who could not participate also supported the Naga peoples mandate to go for Independent country including all the Naga inhabited areas of India and Burma. Ever since the Naga problem not only confined to Naga Hills of Assam but also extended to the free Naga Hills.

After this development, the problem spread throughout the Naga Hills. The Government of India however, maintained that Naga hills are a part of India, which has been inherited from the British India Government. On the contrary, the Nagas asserted that it has never been a part of India, and that the Nagas themselves defended their rights, from the time immemorial, free from any alien rule. They further justified their claim that even during the British colonial rule in India they occupied only some parts of the Naga Hills bordering Assam and Manipur and the rest was called the free Naga Hills. Here the argument arises, this clearly shows that the Britishers had done injustice to the Nagas by handing over the Nagas hills as their own property to the Indian Government. It can thus rightly be concluded that the Naga problem is a legacy of the British Indian Government.

Since the Nagas and the Government of India stood firmly for one right and one wrong, with no meeting points, peace efforts were not successful and remained a pipe dream. It is also argued that the Indian Government was not serious enough to convince the Naga leaders to bring into the fold all contending parties to resolve the problem. Further disagreement with the government of India policy, the Nagas boycotted the first Indian General Elections in 1952. This was followed up by the Nagas launching non-cooperation movement, protesting to withdraw from the Naga Hills. Following this, in 1953, the two Prime Ministers, Jawaharlal Nehru and U Nu of Burma, visited Kohima, to decide the future of the Nagas of India and Burma. But the Nagas walked out from the public meeting where the two leaders were about to give a speech in front of the Nagas. Such unfortunate incident had broken down any chance of negotiation to settle the Naga issue. Thereafter the punitive measures had been taken up to punish the NNC leaders responsible for the incident by the Government. Despite such measures, the Naga leaders went underground to evade the arrest.

Here it may also be pointed out that the situation was largely created by the inefficiency of the Indian political administrative officers, who could not tackle the problems of the situation in the Naga Hills. Their lack of interaction, judgement and observations of the people created the incidence.

Since then in the early part of 1955 the armed confrontation started between the Naga underground and the Indian security forces from the free un-administered Naga Hills of Tuensang frontier areas. Even during the British colonial rule in India, these areas were not included as theirs and the Nagas were not their subjects.

With a view to crush the Naga resistance, the Nehru Government tried to use the military powers to submit the Nagas. But when the Nagas revolted against such policy, the full scale Indo-Naga armed conflicts begun throughout the Naga Hills. To subdue the Nagas underground, extensive operation was launched by the Indian security forces. At the same time they mostly committed atrocities on the civilian Nagas without any justification and also hampered the life of the innocent citizens. The argument is that wrong policy was adopted by using the military power to solve political problem in the name of law and order problem, where as it needed the political solutions. This policy has only aggravated the problems more. The Nagas insurgents started arms and military training from the neighbouring countries to counter the Indian security forces. From this time onward the Naga issue became International, involving neighbours.

However, these confrontationists policy adopted by the Government manoeuvred to win over the educated Nagas and some moderates NNC leaders as well who were protesting against the violent activities in the Naga Hills. Consequent to that, Nagaland State was created in 1963 by carving out the Naga Hills from Assam, Manipur and NEFA. Those few educated people and moderates Nagas were benefited by the creation of State, but the problems added up throughout the Naga Hills. It may be pointed out that if all these areas were placed under administrative control it could have been much easier to solve the Naga Issues. Indeed the new state was created but the problems again multiplied within the Nagas as well as with the Indian Government.

Meanwhile, Peace Mission had initiated a dialogue with the Naga underground and Indo-Naga cease-fire agreement was signed for a political dialogue. But peace talks between the Naga underground leaders and the Government of India failed to reach any concrete solution. The main reason of the deadlock was the Nagas wanted only complete independence whereas the Government of India was not willing to grant complete independence to the Nagas. Other reason was if the Government of India considered the Nagas demand, the vacuum would be created which might prove dangerous to the safety of the Indian security which would be filled by the Indian enemies.

Then came the Shillong Accord of 1975, which was signed by some of the underground leaders with the Government of India. But this too also failed to resolve the problem on the grounds that, (1) the signatories were not the true representatives of the Nagas and (2) The Nagas rejected this Accord. This accord led to further complications not only between the Nagas and the Government of India but also amongst the Naga underground. Consequently, misunderstanding arose and the Naga National Movement got fragmented into different groups. NNC, NSCN and NNC-pro-accord and so on. This factionalism led to further confusion among the Nagas. The consequent mistrust enabled politicians and bureaucrats to ally in some cases patronise a particular factions on specific tribal loyalties, and reinforced tribalism and factionalism.

The Government of India projected the Naga problem as a domestic one. Nevertheless, it involved both India and Burma, politically as well as geographically. For the larger context, the ramification of the Naga movement in both India and Burma involved not only the two big countries but also implicates international actors. The Naga national movement is exploring the possibilities of more and more attention from the International community.

Ethnic conflict can became international on the grounds of:

a) external power involvement,
b) security and strategic considerations,
c) effective humanitarians considerations,
d) irredentism, and
e) if the problems are highlighted by international human rights organization.

Like in the case of the Nagas all these factors are involved. Though the Nagas are divided between two countries, India and Burma the demand for a "Greater Nagaland" is clearly linked with the growing tide of Naga nationalism which have succeeded and transcended the inter-tribe differences and rivalries. The word "Greater Nagaland" includes all the Naga inhabited areas of India and Burma.

The Naga problem is political and not military one and as such it requires political solutions, and should be resolved through peaceful negotiations, mutual understandings and not by armed confrontation. Nagas aspirations and demand cannot be suppressed by armed power nor can the confidence and loyalty be bought through half-hearted developments. This is evident from the continuing Naga problem, which has been going on for the last five decades.

Though there are differences in opinion, many Nagas believe that the elites and the politicians have betrayed the hopes and aspirations of the people. Although these leaders are in a position to steer the destiny of the Nagas, they have failed to take advantage of the Government of India's offer. Moreover, people also feel that the elites and the politicians have rather exploited them by misusing the persisting tribalism for their own personal gains.

Apart from this, the International communities have also not been able to put enough pressure on the government of India, notwithstanding the fact that many Naga lobbies have been able to create an impact in the International forums. Thus, unlike in the erstwhile Soviet Union, the regional power equation in South Asia is disposed of in favour of the Government of India. As a result many Nagas feel that there should be a free and fresh dialogue between the Government of India and all the Naga groups. At the same time, Nagas are also of the opinion that, they should have a right to self-determination, through a path of non-violence.

However there is a clear perception that to solve the Naga problem, the main hindrance is a lack of adequate awareness and agreement with regard, to what it takes to build a nation. The very fact that the state of Nagaland was created manifest, the deep-rooted weakness, distrust, tribalism and division within the Naga movement. The signing of the Shillong Accord in 1975 reflect this inherent weakness.

Some Nagas felt that they should not settle for less than, a protectorate status like Bhutan in South Asia. On the other hand the majority of the Nagas did not want to settle without a Sovereign Independent Nagaland, which include all the Naga inhabited areas of India and Myanmar (Burma). Since, the creation of statehood of Nagaland in 1963, it has excluded the Naga inhabited areas within the Indian dominions as well as Naga who are in Myanmar. This is one of the factors why the problem has not been solved.

In the present context, to settle the Naga problems it is necessary that all the Naga underground factions NSCN (IM) NSCN (K) and NNL (Federal) should participate in any talks or negotiation. . Talks, with one factions of the Nagas underground may not settle the issues as this might again be rejected as the Shillong Accord of 1975, where majority of the Nagas denounced the accord as 'sell out'. Therefore the Nagas in general felt that unification of all the factions are important, to arrive at a consensus on the objective of negotiation to resolve the problem. If all faction unite and agree on the fundamental demands there are strong possibility of final settlement of Naga problem. Inter-tribe rivalries and factional killings will not bring any solution to the Nagas. Therefore to bring all the underground factions NNC, NSCN(IM) and NSCN(K) a Regional Conference is necessary. The organization like Naga Hoho, Church, NGO's NSF (student organization) and also Important Opinion makers and Elders must play an important role in bringing the underground factions. This are part of two-track diplomacy.

Theoretical foundation of the process of negotiations and its methods of analysis span a wide spectrum. Negotiation can be treated as part of a larger system or as an object and process in itself to achieve specific political, economic or other aim. There is no single approach to negotiation. Its reality is apprehended only when approached from any directions, depending upon the types and complexity of issue involved.

Dean Pruitt defines negotiations as process by which a joint discussion is made by two or more parties. The parties first verbalize contradictory demands and then move towards agreement by a process of concession making and a search for new alternatives.[1] Similarly, Zarkman and Berman define it as a "process in which divergent values are combined into an agreed decision, and it is based on the idea that there are appropriate stages, sequences and tactics that can be identified and used to improve the conduct of negotiation and better the chances of success."[2]

Zartman and Berman identifies three stages in the process:

1. Diagnose the situation and decide to try negotiations.
2. Negotiate a formula or common definition of the conflict in terms amenable to a solution.
3. Negotiate the details to implement the formula on precise points of dispute.[3]

Dean Pruitt derive six stages from a synthesis of two of Druckman's.

Based on the theory it indicates that the Naga issue where it could not be able to diagnose the situation for negotiation, to resolve the issues like the creation of statehood in 1963, and the Shillong Accord of 1975. The first stage has been initiated but not properly done. For the second stage there has been an agreement to proceed for negotiation. However, the parties are not able to bring a consensus on the definition of the conflicts in terms of amenable to solution. Moreover all the concern groups are not involved in the negotiation.

The most outstanding characteristic of the disequilibrium in the INDO-NAGA PROBLEMATIQUE is the failure to find a place for Naga values in any of the interrelated projects. The present study is based on our earlier investigation into the history of Naga Peace Ideas and the system of peace values which were reflected in Phizo's personality. It is our contention that although Phizo became the father of Naga Unrest and Revolution, the characteristics of his personality pointed to a balance of attitudes, values and beliefs which could have laid the foundations of a Naga Peace Movement. If India's psyche and political structure had comprehended during his lifetime. Autonomy as a mechanism of mediating relations between the Nagas and New Delhi would have help in finding a solution. Phizo's ideas have a relevance to our contemporary situation, which would include:

- Human Rights
- Elimination of inter-tribal rivalry
- Cultural and educational advancement of Nagas
- Naga self determination/self administration
- India's security concerns
- Global socio-economic policy
- Global and regional disarmament
- Nonviolence verses syndrome of force and the Nagas
- The Church as the centre of social and political power and preservation of peace and freedom
- Mechanism of international coordination

It is distressing to observe how a sophisticated democracy like India continued to define in controversial terms. Phizo's peace-related thinking, judgement and expectations. At a time when major shift took place in European peace research in favour of Gandhian and Indian peace-related ideas, New Delhi in its interactions with Phizo subordinated peace values to values of stabilization which engendered collective aggressiveness on both sides. The result it was decodes of social injustice and political instability among the Naga people. Phizo, on the contrary understood that Naga social reality was formed by tribes, which in turn were formed by persons in a "conscious process of free action". Both at home and from exile in Britain, he exhorted his followers to respect the rights of the human person to act on behalf of peace both on account of Naga tribal peace values and on account of Christian personalism. It is a continuing fallacy of the Indian bureaucracy to see the Naga problem through the prism of insurgency and violence like in other parts of the country and the world and not to build upon the ideals of Naga tribal humanism and Christian personalism which were always espoused by Phizo when he defended social peace and condemned repression.

If India is to pursue a vision appropriate to the 21 century, the Naga problem should not remain locked in misguided bureaucratic policies, but should be approached on the basis of moral confidence in the Naga people. The imperatives of a new approach should include:

1. A mandate for making arrangement acceptable to all Naga groups to discuss possibilities that would allow them to sign an interim agreement for autonomy of self-government.
2. A series of unilateral acts by the Government of India to show that they recognise the "historical and inalienable" rights of the Naga people and are willing to create a situation of trust which would move the peace process forward.
3. A series of Confidence Building Measures under the auspices of an autonomous Naga people's Development Organisation (NPDO).
4. The NPDO would have full powers over allocation of financial, fiscal, investment and human resources, and also have an international technical support network.
5. A wide range of positive proposals would be developed during the interim period which would be "functional" and would be in four baskets:

    a) Political
    b) Strategic
    c) Commercial and industrial
    d) Free movement of the Naga people in the traditional Naga territories across territorial borders

6. To separate the issue of "sovereignty" from the issues of "self-administration" till the time when final talks are held. During the period of interim talks a non-confrontational relationship will be created by creating a balance between the Naga interests and the interests of the Government of India.
7. The International Covenant of Civil and Political Rights and the International Covenant on Economic, Social and Cultural Rights will be reiterated by both sides.
8. Naga political activism will not be inhibited by the bureaucratic machine, although the question of sovereignty in relation to other states will not be a issue in the interim period. The focus will be on (a) Naga local security (2) Naga regional stability (c) Naga environmental security and (d) Naga regional political, economic and social networks.

9. To formulate a Naga Charter incorporating the political legacy of Phizo and the new thinking among the Naga intelligentsia and to provide effective tools in the hands of Naga civil society with the following basic assumption:
   i. Resurrection of Naga self-respect
   ii. Maintenance of Naga strategic strength against potential risks
   iii. Transition to mutual arms reduction talks and ability to secure political agreements without resort to weapons
   iv. Rehabilitation of the Naga economy
   v. Expansion of cooperation with cross border Naga communities
   vi. Transition to partnership relations between political, bureaucratic and military and paramilitary formations
   vii. General expansion of cooperation in ensuring mutual security through creation and projection of images of peace and friendship based on Naga peace values.
10. Final talks to realise new structures and processes outside the present constitutional context.

REFERENCES

1. Dean J. Pruitt, *Negotiational Behaviour, New York: Academic Press,* 1981, p. 1.
2. I.W. Zartman and M.R. Berman, *The Practical Negotiator,* New Haven, Yale University Press, 1982, p. VII–VIII.
3. Zartman & Berman, Ibid., p. 9.

Chronology of Naga Political Development

The Naga History

1832–1997

1832: First contacts between the British and the Nagas, when Captain Jenkins and Lieutenant Pemberton escorted by Raja Gumbeer Sing's Manipur troops forced a passage through.

1855: Colonel McCulloch's policy of planting Kuki settlements on exposed frontiers. A large colony of Kukis (collective noun for several tribes from the south) were settled in the neibourhood of Longing to act as a barrier for North Cachar against the raids of the Angami Nagas.

1879: The British conquered parts of Naga territory and called the area "Naga Hills" and the inhabitants "subjects Nagas". The Nagas outside this area were "Free Nagas".

1880: Kukis continued their campaign to decimate the Naga population and plunder their wealth with firearms supplied by the British and the Kingdom of Manipur.

1918: Formation of the Naga Club, a union of western-educated Nagas.

1929: 10 January, the British subjects Nagas demanded Independence when the India Statutory Commission (under the Chairmanship of Sir John Simon) visited Kohima, asking the Nagas whether they would join the coming "New Reform" which afterwards became the government of India Act of 1935.

1936: Naga Hills allowed to remain "Excluded Area" outside the Indian Constitution Act, 1935.

1939: 1 April, British District "Naga Hills" declared as "Naga Hills Excluded Area" under the Government of India (Excluded and Partially Excluded area). Order 1936, and have since the 1st of April 1937 been administered by the Governor, in his discretion as the agent of the Government the British-India Empire.

1944: Jawarharlal Nehru has taken a stand in the support of self determination of the Nagas: "...It may be desirable to fix a period of say ten years later after the establishment of the Free Indian State at the end of which the right of secede may be exercised through a proper constitutional process and in accordance with the clearly expressed will be the inhabitants of the area concerned."

April, Naga involved in World War II. The Colonial Liberation Front along with the Japanese Imperial Army reached Kohima. Nagas were deeply involved in the fight. Some fought on the side of the Japanese, others fought on the side of the Allies. (Both sides honestly and sincerely believed that they were fighting for own national liberty, freedom and independence).

1946: February, The Nagas formed a full-fledged political organ, the Naga National Council (NNC). Mr. T. Aliba Imti became the 1st President of the NNC.

9 April, the British Cabinet Mission was sent to India. The NNC informed this mission that Naga future would not be bound by any arbitrary decision of the British Government and that the Nagas would not accept any recommendation.

August, Nehru's letter to the NNC: "It is obvious that the Naga territory in eastern Assam is too small to stand by itself politically and economically. It lies between the two countries, India and China, and a part of it consists of rather backward people who require considerable help."

20 August, Mr. and Mrs. A. Omeo Kumar Das, Indian Congress leaders, came to Kohima and visited surround-

ing villages. They were the first even Indian leaders who visited Nagaland.

December, the NNC was urged and warned in its Mokokchung Winter Session to hurry up for Naga Independence or else the Nagas would be involved in a war which would be unnecessary and costly for the Nagas.

1947: 20 February, The Nagas demanded an Interim Government (Guardian power), effected prior to the British departure, for a period of ten years and self-determination there after.

May, second memorandum submitted for the guardian power with further details and clarification.

19–21 May, "Sub-committee of the Constitution Assembly of the Government of India" under the Chairmanship of Shri. Gopinath Bardoloi visited Kohima. The Naga political affairs were discussed with NNC for three days.

May, The NNC called upon Assam to form a sovereign state of Assam.

26 June, Assam Governor Sir Akbar Hydari came to Kohima to solve the Naga political problem. A memorandum was submitted to him. He proposed and submitted a plan for the "10 years agreement" (=Nine-point or Hydari Agreement). The NNC agreed with modification for self determination at the end of this period.

11 July, The Deputy Commissioner in Kohima informed the NNC that the "Prime Minister of India has agreed to substance of agreement with Nagas made by the Governor".

19 July, Naga delegation met Mahatma Gandhi in New Delhi (Bhangi Colony), and informed him of the decision by the Nagas to declare Independence.

14 August, Independence declared by the subject Nagas of the excluded areas (Southern Nagas including Manipur Nagas and Chachar Nagas with Knoyak Nagas). The Government of India and the United Nations were informed by cable.

15 August, Independence of India. The Indian administration tried to hoist the flag in some parts of the Naga areas including Kohima, but the flags were brought down immediately by the Nagaas making their feelings clear.

1948: 9 May, Two men Naga delegation met H.E. Governor of Assam Sir, Akbar Hydari, Shillong, to ascertain the position of the "ten years agreement". The Governor said: "The agreement had been incorporated in the sixth schedule of the constitution of India". The Nagas took the agreement on the basis of a treaty. (The agreement turned out to be a false document).

11 June, The 10 year agreement's full implementation again assured by the Shillong office under memo 490/C-Shillong.

22 June, "10 year agreement" signed in Shillong by H.E. the Governor of Assam and the premier of Assam (Memo No. 88-c/47-570-72) Shillong.

1949: 8 November, A three men Naga delegation met the representatives of the Government of India in Shillong to ascertain the actual position of the 10 year agreement. This agreement between NNC and Government of India was now officially repudiated. (q-v-11 and 22 June, 1945).

28 November, A 11-men Naga delegation went to New Delhi to meet the Governor General of Free India, Shri C. Rajagopalachari, in Shillong. His Excellency said, "Nagas are at full liberty to become independent, if they felt it would be in their interest".

30 December, The NNC, which was now the administrative authority in the Naga hills excluded area, announced a Sovereign state of Nagaland and to be established at the earliest possible date.

1950: 9 January, A four men delegation went to New Delhi to meet the Governor General of Free India. An interview was refused by the External Ministry. The delegation was told to meet the Assam Governor.

14 January, The delegation returned and went to Shillong to meet the Governor of Assam, Shri. Prakash by the External Ministry in New Delhi. Again was said that the Nagas were at full liberty to become independent outside of the Indian Union. The delegation informed that the Indian Constitution cannot bind the Nagas even when it became law in India.

24 January, The NNC informed the Govt. of India, United Nations and all the Foreign Ambassadors in New Delhi that the Nagas do not accept the Indian Constitution.

18 February, No Naga representative to be sent to the Indian Union Assemblies or Parliament.

8 May, The Government of India called the Nagas to set up "District Autonomy."

25 May, The NNC informed the Indian Government that the Nagas will not accept 'District Autonomy".

29 June, The new Assam Governor Mr. Jairamdas Doulatram, paid his first visit to Kohima.

16 October, The Indian Government sent Assam Oil Co. to Chumukedima for exploitation of oil in Nagaland. A 50 men Naga representatives met the Assam Oil Co. The company was requested not to proceed with the oil drilling operations.

A press report revealed that the Indian Government received from A.O.C a sum of Rs. 30 million as royalty for exploitation of oil in Nagaland.

27 October, A twelve men Naga delegations went to Shillong to meet the Indian President Dr. Rajendra Prasad, on his first visit to Assam, Capital Shillong. The Assam Government refused to the interview. So a memorandum was submitted to the president through Assam Chief Minister Shri. Bisnuram Medhi.

30 October, Letter sent to the President of India informing him of the Naga stands for National Independence along with a letter dated 27 October.

31 October, Letter of protest sent to the President of India for his "constitution (removal of difficulties) Order" issued on 27 October, 1950, New Delhi and against the nomination of a representative in the Indian Parliament for the free Nagas.

6–8 December, Chief Minister of Assam, Mr. B. Medhi, came to Kohima and Mokokchung. He was told in the Public meeting that Nagas would become independent.

1951: 1 January, Government of India informed Naga voluntary plebiscite for Naga Independence.

26 January, Protest lodged to Assam Oil Co. and a copy sent to the other authorities concerned, and to the United Nations for information and record.

28 February, Protest lodged to the Governor of Assam (3).

30 March, Letter sent to the President of India requesting to sent an Indian Government representative as observer of the voluntary plebiscite (which is organised by the NNC).

16 May, The Voluntary Plebiscite commenced. Result 99.9% in favour of a sovereign state, Assam Governor Shri. Jairamdas Doulatram visited Nagaland. Memorandum for independence submitted to him.

7 July, A nine men Naga delegation met Shri. Prakash, former Assam Governor, the Indian Cabinet Minister for scientific research and Natural Resources, New Delhi, camp Shillong. The Naga problem is discussed.

19 December, A twenty three men Naga delegation went to Shillong and asked the Governor of Assam Shri. Jairamdas Doulatram, to forward the result of the Naga Voluntary Plebiscite (99-9/10 in favour of independence) to the Government of India, New Delhi. He refused.

1952: 25 January, First General election of free India started. The Naga did not participate in the Indian election.

11 March, A three men Naga delegation of the NNC (under President A.Z. Phizo) met the Prime Minister of

India Mr. Nehru in New Delhi. The result of the Naga Voluntary Plebiscite of the thumb impressions was submitted to the President of India.

21 April, Letter sent to the United Nations. Submitted the resolution of the NNC, April 12, 1952.

16 May, Jawarharlal Nehru, Prime Minister of India, was invited to visit Nagaland.

21 July, An order came out to arrest the President of the NNC, A.Z. Phizo. Advance information was received and the arrest was (now) avoided.

14 August, decision taken (by the NNC) to have no link whatever with the Indian Administration.

18 October, Zasibito (Jotsoma) a Naga leader and Asstt. Judge, Court of KCC, is killed by an Indian Officer on the main road of Kohima.

24 October, Prime Minister of India Mr. Nehru came to Mao, a border Naga village.

1953: 3 March, The Prime Ministers of India and Burma, Mr. Nehru and Mr. U. Nu, came to Kohima and was welcomed by the Naga representatives. More than 10,000 Nagas came in the meeting. Nehru's attitude was not one of openness. He did not try to find out the wishes of the Naga people. He wanted to tell them what they should do. An interview was not allowed by any order on the spot. In protest the Naga elders walked out of the reception.

April, The Indian Government resorted to serve political persecution, mass arrest, torture and terrorism against the Nagas. The Assam Maintenance of Public Order (Autonomous Districts) Act 1953 was introduced.

13 April, An instruction was given to the Indian Armed Forces in Nagaland. A letter of Protest was sent to the Prime Minister of India against this abominable instruction.

29 May, The Indian Armed Forces (reported to 1200) attacked Khonoma village (550 housed).

8 September, Decision taken (by NNC) that the Nagas would not be the first party to move for seeking negotiation with India.

9 September, The Indian Government formulated a new regulation of "Forced Labour" upon the Nagas and introduced in Nagaland, signed by the President of India. Any Naga refusing to carry the Indian Cooly loads is punishable with imprisonment for one year or fine of Rs. 500/- with both.

21–3, September, Mr. Bimlaprasad Chaliha, President of the Assam Pradesh Congress Committee, came to study the situation in Nagaland.

29 September, Naga GBS resigned in protest of the 'forced labour' regulation.

1–14 October, The Praja Socialist Party, (Assam) Good Will Mission came to Nagaland and visited all the principal areas of Kohima and Mokokchung Divisions.

30 November to 15 December, Naga Good Will Mission to Assam. It visited Assam and toured throughout Assam state as guest of the Congress.

2 December, In a speech B. Medhi, Chief Minister of Assam said: "I cannot think of any demand for an independent sovereign Naga state raised by a handful of Naga leaders, mostly Christian. And probably this demand was raised by interested foreign missionaries to keep them isolated from the rest of India."

2 January, A speaker of the Indian Parliament, Shri. G.V. Navalankar, came to Kohima. A Naga delegation met him and told him the Naga stand of National Independence.

Rajkumari Armit Kaur, Health Minister of the Government of India, came to Imphal. A Naga delegation interviewed her. She was one of those women leader present when a Naga delegation met Mahatma Gandhi on July 19 July, 1947.

4 July, the Naga Supreme Court is established.

15 November, The Indian Armed Forces resorted to massacre in "Free Naga" territory.

1954: The Assam Disturbed Areas Act(1955) is introduced to enable the Assam Armed Police (AP) and Assam Rifles to execute their tasks openly without legal constraints. The number of Naga men and women tortured and sexually assaulted multiplied.

6 March, A Naga women delegation went to Shillong to meet the Governor Mr. Jairamdas Doulatram and the Chief Minister Mr. B. Medhi. Their mission was to explain the situation in Nagaland and to seek a solution to stop the atrocities that had been going on for months.

25 March, Fighting between the Free Naga Government forces and the Indian Army started.

30 March, Protest against mass massacre of free Nagas was sent to the Indian Government, Foreign Ambassadors in New Delhi, Queen of the UK, American President and the Secretary of the State, and the United Nations.

31 March, The Vice President of NNC sent the following cable to the United Nations, with copies to the Government of India and all foreign Ambassadors in New Delhi: "Report reaching Kohima say that more than ten thousand men, women and children of Free Nagas believed to have been already killed by the Indian troops within the few days of wholesale massacre stop people are being systematically from village to village in Free Nagaland stop urgently appeal to you in the name of humanity to intervene and stop killing".

27 April, No political party of a foreign character will be introduced into Nagaland. (but NNC)

7 May, States Re-Organisation Commission (SRC) of the Govt. of India visited Kohima. A Naga delegation of 50 people met the Commission and explained to them the stand of the Nagas for National Independence. A memorandum was submitted. (An Order of arrest of the President of the NNC was lifted on request and he was with the delegation).

13 August, A Naga Mission of Assam, Mr. B. Medhi. A pledge for Peace was signed and both the NNC and the Govt. promised to help each other.

25 August, The Naga Mission of Peace again went to Shillong and met Assam Chief Minister Mr. Medhi because of the situation, which was developing in a more serious nature. The Nagas of the Naga Hills Excluded Area had not involved themselves so far in the fight against the free Nagas. But the Indian Authority started using force to carry and transport their war material to Nagaland.

26 November, The Indian National Congress President, Shri. U.N. Dhebar, came to Kohima via Imphal. Earlier, the Assam Congress President, Mhadra Mohan Chaudhury and Shri, Man Prafulla Goswami MLA came and appealed to the Nagas to welcome the Indian Congress President. A complete arrangement was made for a rousing welcome but the local authority wrecked it again.

1955: Start of the "village grouping policy" by the Indian Government. Village after village was uprooted and shifted to new locations—called "village grouping area". (These areas were in fact concentration camps. People had no freedom and no place or time for the cultivation of crops.)

14 January, the Naga constitution (The Yehzabo) is approved by the NNC.

22 March, the Naga Federal Government inaugurated by the NNC. In two months time it raised a standing army, the "Naga Home Guard".

24 March, The first clash took place between the Naga Home Guard (Naga Federal Forces) and the Indian Army.

1956: June, The IB officer Dutt convened a meeting of the moderate Naga leaders, and named it the "Working Committee Meeting" for calling a convention in August. From these meetings the so-called Naga People's Convention was formed.

23 August, The first Naga People's Convention (NPC) at Kohima.

1 December, The Naga Hills and Tuensang Area (NHTA) is made an autonomous district under a Commissioner. (The Tuensang Division is taken out of the North East Frontier Agency (NEFA)).

1957: The years of the introduction of two special laws to oppress the Naga Revolt.

21 May, The Second Naga People's Convention at Ungma.

September, The Special Power Ordinance (1958) is converted into an Act. (The Armed Forces (Assam and Manipur) Special Powers Act).

1958: The Third People's Convention at Mokokchung. The Convention accepted the draft for a new Agreement with the Indian Government (See later: The Sixteenth Point Agreement) which was prepared by a drafting committee.

1959: July, The final draft of the Third Naga People's Convention (NPC) is materialised as the Sixteenth Point Agreement between the NPC and the Government of India. It emphasised that the minimum demand would be full Statehood within the Indian Union.

1962: The Nagaland Security Regulation, 1962 is introduced.

1963: The Nagaland and Nationalist Organization (NNO), is established. It arose from the NPC. Some supporters of the NNC established the Democratic Party of Nagaland.

1 December, Nagaland is declared to be a full fledged state of the Indian Union by Article 371A of the Constitution of India and Under the External Affairs Ministry of Govt. of India.

1964: 6 September, "Peace day": Cease fire between the Naga Federal Forces and the Indian Army.

1965: 22 November, Jaya Prakash Narayan suggested in the parliament that "it is far more important to have friendly Nagas on our frontier closely associated with us in some new constitutional manner rather than unfriendly and discontented Nagas kept forcibly within the Indian Union". Immediately many members of the Parliament demanded his arrest.

1968: 6 March, Launch of the amended Yehzabo of Nagaland.

11 July, Atrocities at Yankeli village. A tragedy of bloody sexual debauchery perpetrated by the 8th Mountain Division of the Indian Army at the consecrated pulpit of the Yankeli Baptist Christian Church.

1972: The Special Powers Act, 1958 is amended as the Armed Forces Special Act (1972) to make it applicable to all states and Union territories in the North-East.

31 August, The government of India declared that the NNC, the Federal Government of Nagaland and its Army (the Federal Army) were "unlawful associations" under the unlawful activities (prevention) Act, no. 37 of 1967.

1975: 11 November, Shillong Accord was signed, between the Government of India and the NNC Federal Government Representative.

1976: 5 January, Annexure "G" Supplementary Agreement to the Shillong Accord. (= Implementation of Clause II of the Shillong Accord).

1978: 9 September, The Naga People's Movement for Human Rights (NPMHR) is formed in response to the Naga People's long feel need for an organisation movement to protect and further their Human Rights.

1979: 20 July, The students organised demonstration in five centres in the Chakhesang-district which was joined by representatives of the Naga student's federation. The specific demand of the students is the removal of the 14 Battalion of the Assam Rifles from the area.

1980: 31 January, The Nationalist Socialist Council of Nagaland (NSCN) established by the former members of the NNC, Isak Chishi Swu and The. Muivah. (They are now resp. Chairman and General Secretary of the NSCN) The NSCN will use the armed struggle as mean to reach their goal: A Sovereign Naga State.

1981: 28–29 August, The Naga National Workers, (NNW) met at a general meeting in Kohima. This meeting under the sessional Chairmanship of Gen. Thinosielie Medon Keyho is considered to be one of the biggest gatherings of the Nagas held after the "Shillong Accord" as it was represented by all Naga Nationalities. The Shillong Accord is "Condemned and abrogated". The other objective of the NNW conference (NNWC) is to work for the Naga National Unity.

1986: July, Presentation of Naga Case to USA by General Mowu.

4–7 August Gen. Mowu Gwizan, Representative of the NNWC participated in the UN Working Group on Indigenous Peoples at Geneva.

1988: Division in the NSCN. There are now two NSCN-factions: The Swu & Muivah faction and the S.S. Khaplang faction.

1990: 30 April, Death of Mr. A.Z. Phizo, the exiled NNC President.

1 May, Ms. Adino Phizo, the daughter of Mr. A.Z. Phizo, is made NNC acting president by the 'Shillong Accordist' in the NNC. She is not accepted, as president, by the NNC members who condemned the Shillong Accord. They will choose another president (see 17 July).

17 July, Mr. Khodao Yanthan (of the Lotha tribe) is elected as the new president of the NNC after he returned from his London exile.

10–18 September, NNC Convention at Wokha. Mr. Khodao Yanthan held his elect Speech. His task is to 'seek for Naga Unity and peace'. The policy of the NNC will continued to be: "To face the Indian Government in the open ground in Non-violence and non cooperation through a democratic process as a Nation to a Nation..."

1991, 8 November, UK based Human Rights Groups 'Naga Vigil' David Ward and Stephen Hillman arrived in Nagaland to study the Political Situation and Human Rights Violation by the Indian Armed Forces

1993: 23 January, The NSCN (Swu and Muivah faction) became a member of the Underrepresented Nations and People Organisation (UNPO). The NNC (Khodao & Mowu) has tried twice to applicate for the membership. Their letters (seemed to have) never arrived at the UNPO–office at the Hague (Deng Haag), Rob Vermeulen (NCIV) August, 1993.

1997 28 July, to 3 August, Atlanta meeting Georgia in (USA) Appeal for reconciliation of the Naga underground faction for a Peaceful resolution of the conflict.

1 August, Cease-fire declaration between the Government of India and NSCN (IM).

2001 June. Extension of Ceasefire upto 31st July 2002 (IM)

2001 28th April, Cease-fire declaration between the Government of India and NSCN(K) for one year.

APPENDIX I

To,
The Indian Statutory Commission,
Camp India

MEMORANDUM ON THE NAGA HILLS

Sir,

We the undersigned Naga of the Naga Club at Kohima who are the only persons at present who can voice for our people have heard with great regret that our Hill included within the Reformed Schemes of India without our knowledge, but as the administration of our Hills continued to be in the hands of the British Officers we did not consider it necessary to raise any protest in the past. Now, we learn that you have come to India as representatives to British Government to enquire into the working of the system of Government and the growth of education and we beg to submit below our view with the prayer that our Hills may be withdrawn from the Reformed Scheme and placed outside the Reforms Schemes but directly under British Government. We never asked for any reforms and we don't wish for any reforms.

Before the British Government conquered our Country in 1879–1880, we were living in a state of intermittent warfare with Assamese of the Assam Valley to the North and West of our country and the Manipur is to the South. They never conquered us, nor were we subjected to their rule. On the other hand, we were always a terror to those people. Our country within the administered area consists of more than eight tribes, quite different from one another with quite different languages which cannot be understood by each other, and there are more tribes outside the administered area which are not known at present. We have no unity among us and it is only the British Government that is holding us together now.

Our education at present is poor. The occupation of our country by the British Government being so recent in 1880, we have had no choice or opportunity to improve in education and though we can boast of two or three graduates of an Indian University in our country, we have not got one yet who is able to represent all our different tribes or master our languages much loss one to represent us in any council of a province. Moreover, our population numbering 102000 is very small in comparison with the population of the plain districts in the province, and any representation that may be allotted to us in the council will be negligible and we will have no weight whatsoever.

Our country is poor and it does not pay for its administration. Therefore, if it is continued to be placed under the reformed Scheme, we are afraid that now and then heavy taxes will have to be imposed on us and when we cannot pay them all lands will have to be sold and in the long run we shall have no share in the land of our birth and life will not be worth living then. Though our land at present is within the British territory, Government have always recognised our private rights in tax, but if we are forced to enter the council of the majority all these rights may be extinguished by unsympathetic council, the majority of whose number is sure to belong to the plain district. We also have much fear the introduction of foreign laws and customs to supersede our customary laws which we now enjoy.

For the above reasons, we pray that the British Government will continue to safeguard our rights against all encroachment from other people who are more advanced than us by withdrawing our country from the Reformed Scheme and placing it directly under its own protection. If the British Government however, want to throw us away, we pray that we should not be thrust to the mercy of the people who could never subjugate us, but to leave us alone to determine for ourselves as in ancient times. We claim (not only the members of the Nagas Club) to represent all these tribes to which we belong: Angamis, Kacha Nagas, Kukis, Semas, Lothas, and Rengmas.

Signed by:

Nihu, Head Interpretor Angami.
Nisalo Peshkas, Angami.
Nisher, Master, Angami.
Khosa, Doctor, Angami.
Gepo, Interpretor, Kacha Naga.
Vipunyu, Potdar, Angami.
Goyiepra, Treasure, Angami.
Rushukhrie, Master, Angami.
Zupulhoulie, Master, Angami.
Dkhrie, Sub-overseer, Angami.
Zopulie, Interpretro, Angami.
Lengjang, Interetor, Kuki.
Nikhriehu, Interpretor, Angami.
Miakrao, Chprasi. Angami.
Levi, Clerk, Kacha Naga.
Katsumo, Interpretor, Angami.
Nuolhoukelie, Clerk, Angami.
Luzevi, Sema, Interpretor.
Apamo, Interpretor, Lotha.
Resilo, Interpretor, Kuki.

Dated the 26th March, 1928/10-1-1929.

APPENDIX II

THE HYDARI AGREEMENT

The Nine Point Agreement (The Hydari Agreement) Arrived at Between The Naga National Council and The Governor of Assam In June, 1947.

1. Judicial

All cases whether civil or criminal arising between Nagas in the Naga Hills will be deposed of by duly constituted Naga courts according to Naga customary law, or such law as may be introduced with the consent of duly recognised Naga representative organisation, save that where a sentence of transportation or death has been passed there will be right of appeal to the Governor.

In cases arising between Nagas and non Naga in (a) Kohima and Mikokchung areas, and (b) in the neighbouring plains districts, the judge if not a Naga, will be assisted by the Naga assessor.

2. Executive

The general principles is accepted that what the Naga National Council is prepared to pay for the Naga National Council should control. This principle will apply to the work done as well as the staff employed.

While the District Officer will be appointed at the discretion of the Governor, Sub-divisional Council with a full time executive president, paid by the Naga National Council, who would be responsible to the District Officers, for all matters falling within the latter's responsibility, and to the Naga National Council for all matters falling within their responsibility.

In Regard to

a) Agriculture: The Naga National Council will exercise all the powers now vested in the District Officer.
b) PWD: The Naga National Council will take over full control.
c) Education and Forest Department: The Naga National Council is prepared to pay for all the services and staff.

3. Legislative

That no laws passed by the provincial or Central Legislature which would materially affect the terms of this agreement of the religious practices of the Naga shall have legal force in the Naga Hills without the consent of the Naga National Council.

In cases of dispute as to whether any law did so affect this agreement , the matter would be referred by the Naga National Coucil to the Governor who would then direct that the law in question should not have legal force in the Naga Hills pending the decision of the Central Government.

4. Land

That land with all its resources in the Naga Hills should not be alienated to a non-Naga without the consent of the Naga National Council.

5. Taxation

That the Naga National Council will be responsible for the imposition, collection, and expenditure of land revenue and house tax, and of such other taxes as may be imposed by the Naga National Council.

6. Boundaries

That present administrative divisions should be modified so as to (1) bring back into the Naga Hills District all the forest transferred to the Sibsagar and Nowgong District in the past, and (2) bring under one unified administrative unit, as far as possible, all Nagas. All the areas so included would be within the scopes of the present proposed agreement.

No areas should be transferred out of the Naga Hills without the consent of the Naga National Council.

7. Arms Act

The District Officer will act on the advice of the Naga National Council in accordance with the provision of the Arms Act.

8. Regulations

The Chin Hills Regulations and the Bengal Eastern Frontier Regulations will remain in force.

9. Period of Agreement

The Governor of Assam as the agent of the Government of Indian Union will have a special responsibility for a period of ten years to ensure the due observance of this agreement; at the end of this period the Naga National Council will be asked whether they require the above agreement to be extended for a further period, or a new agreement regarding the future of the Naga people arrived at.

Naga National Council Response

Telegram sent to the Indian Government on 14 August 1947, *"Naga hills cannot be considered part of Indian Union until heads of proposed agreement between Governor of Assam and the Naga National Council are accepted to the letters of execution, with the clause nine modified as, 'the end of this period the Naga will be free to decide their future'."*

Governor and Chief Minister of Assam's Written Assurance about Implementation of the Hydari Agreement

A deputation of Naga gentlemen have come to Shillong to receive a written assurance from H.E. the Governor of Assam and the Honourable Premier, to the effect that the agreement reached between His Excellency and the Naga leaders in June 1947 will be implemented. The deputation was given an assurance by both that there was never any question of non implementation of the agreement. A misunderstanding appeared to have arisen in the minds of certain sections of the Naga people that the agreement of June, 1947, was nullified by the provision laid down in the Draft Constitution. It was explained to the deputation, at length, the Draft constitution was in no way inconsistent with the agreement. On the contrary, it prescribed the machinery whereby the agreement might be translated into action. If, however, there still remained any doubt or apprehension in the minds of the Naga people, regarding the validity of the agreement, H.E. and the Honourable Premier were prepared to give the written assurance that had been asked for. They have been pleased to do so accordingly and both have appended their signature to this document as a token of the assurance they have been asked to give.

APPENDIX III

THE SIXTEEN POINT AGREEMENT

The Sixteen Point Agreement Arrived At Between The Naga People's Convention and The Government of India in July, 1960.

The point placed by the delegates of the Naga People's Convention before the Prime Minister on 26 July 1960, as finally recast by the delegation in the light of discussions on 27, and 28 July, 1960, with the Foreign Secretary.

1. The Name

The territories that were heretofore known as the Naga Hills Tuensang Area under the Naga Hills Tuensang Area Act 1957, shall or a State within the Indian Union and be hereafter known as Nagaland.

2. The Ministry In Charge

The Nagaland shall be under the Ministry of External affairs of the Government of India.

3. The Governor of Nagaland

1) The President of India shall appoint a Governor for Nagaland and he will be vested with the executive powers of the Government of Nagaland. He will have his headquarters in Nagaland.
2) His administrative secretariat will be headed by a Chief Secretary stationed at the Headquarters with other Secretariat Staff as necessary.

3) The Governor shall have special responsibility with regard to law and order during the transitional period and for so long as the law and order situation continues to remain disturbed on account of hostile activities. In exercising this special responsibility, the Governor shall, after consultation with the Ministry, act in his individual judgement. This special responsibility of the Governor will cease when normalcy returns.

4. Council of Ministers

1) There shall be a Council of Ministers with a Chief Minister at the head to assist and advise the Governor in the exercise of his functions.
2) The Council of Ministers shall be responsible to the Naga Legislative Assembly.

5. The Legislature

There shall be constituted a Legislative Assembly consisting of elected and nominated members as may be deemed necessary representing different Tribes. (Further a duly constituted body of Experts may be formed to examine and determine the principles of representation and democratic basis).

6. Representation in Parliament

Two elected members shall represent Nagaland in the Union Parliament, that is to say one for the Lok Sabha and the other for, the Rajya Sabha.

7. Acts of Parliament

No act or law passed by the Union Parliament affecting the following provision shall have legal force in Nagaland unless specifically applied to it by a majority vote of the Nagaland Legislative Assmbly.

1) The Religious or Social Practices of the Nagas.
2) Naga Customary Laws and Procedure.

3) Civil and Criminal Justice so far as these concern decision according to Naga Customary Law. The existing laws relating to administration of civil and criminal justice as provided in the Rules for the Administration of Justice and Police in the Naga Hills District shall continue to be in force.
4) The ownership and transfer of land and its resources.

8. Local Self-Government

Each tribes shall have the following units of rule making and administrative local bodies to deal with matters concerning the respective tribes and areas.

1) The Village Council
2) The Range Council and
3) The Tribal Council

This Council will also deal with disputes and cases involving breaches of customary laws and usages.

9. Administration of Justice

a) The existing system of administration of civil and criminal Justice shall continue.
b) Appallate Course
    1) The District Court cum Session Court, (for each district), High Court and Supreme Court of India.
    2) The Naga Tribunal (for the whole of the Nagaland) in respect of cases decided according to customary law.

10. Administration of Tuensang District

1) The Governor shall carry on the administration of the Tuensang District for a period of 10 (ten) years until such time when the tribes in the Tuensang District are capable of shouldering more responsibility of the advanced system of administration. The commencement of the ten-year period of administration will start simultaneously with

the enforcement of detailed workings of the constitution in other parts of the Nagaland.

2) Provided further that a Regional Council shall be formed for Tuensang District by elected representatives from all the tribes in Tuensang District, and the Governor may nominate representatives to the Regional council, as well. The Deputy Commissioner will be the Ex-officio Chairman of the Council. The Regional Council will elect members to Naga Legislative Assembly to represent Tuensang District.
3) Provided further that for the advice of the Regional Council, steps will be taken to start various councils and Courts, in those areas where the people feel themselves capable of establishing such institutions.
4) Provided further that no Act or Law passed by the Naga Legislative Assembly shall be applicable to Tuensang District unless specifically recommended by the Regional Council.
5) Provided further that the Regional Council shall supervise and guide the working of the various Councils and Tribal Courts within Tuensang District and wherever necessary depute the local officers to act as Chairman thereof.
6) Provided further that council of such areas inhabited by a mixed population or which have not as yet decided to which specific Tribal Council to be affiliated to shall be directly under the Regional Council for the time being. And at the end of ten years the situation will be reviewed and if the people so desire the period will be further extended.

11. Financial Assistance from the Government of India

To supplement the revenue of the Nagaland, there will be need for the Government of India to pay out of the Consolidation Fund of India.

1) A lump sum each year for the development progress in Nagaland; and
2) A grant-in-aid towards meeting the cost of administration.

Proposals for the above grants shall be prepared and submitted by the Government of Nagaland to the Government of India for their approval. The governor will have general responsibility for ensuring that the funds made available by the Government of India are expended for purposes for which they have been approved.

12. Consolidation of Forest Areas

The delegation wished the following to be placed on record:

The Naga delegation discussed the question of the inclusion of the reserve forests of contiguous areas inhabited by the Nagas. They were referred to the provisions in Articles 3 and 4 of the Constitution, prescribing the procedure for the transfer of areas from one State to another.

13. Consolidation of Contiguous Naga Areas

The delegation wished the following to be placed on record:

The Naga leaders expressed the wish for the contiguous areas to join the new state. It was pointed out to them on behalf of the Government of India that Articles 3 and 4 of the Constitution provided for increasing the area of any State, but that is was not possible for the Government of India to make any commitment in this regard at this stage.

14. Formation of Separate Naga Regiment

In order that the Naga people can fulfil their desire of playing a full role in the defence forces of India the question of raising a separate Naga Regiment should be duly examined for action.

15. Transitional Period

a) On reaching the political settlement with the Government of India, the Government of India will prepare a Bill for such amendment of the Constitution, as may be necessary, in order to implement the decision, The Draft Bill, before presentation to Parliament, will be shown to the delegates of the NPC.

b) There shall be constituted an Interim Body with elected representatives from every tribes, to assist and advise the Governor in the administration of the Nagaland during the transitional period. The tenure of office of the Interim Body will be 3 (three) years subject to re-election.

16. Inner Line Regulation

Rule embodied in the Bengal Eastern Frontier Regulation, 1873, shall remain in force in the Nagaland.

APPENDIX IV

BILATERAL AGREEMENT ON CEASE-FIRE

The order took effect since September, 1964.

TERMS

1. Government of India

On the understanding that the Government of India will undertake to suspend:

a) Jungle Operation;
b) Raiding of Federal Army and Administrative camps;
c) Patrolling not beyond 1000 yards, of security posts;
d) Searching of villages;
e) Aerial Actions;
f) Imposition of forced labour (on the people);
g) Imposition of Fine (political).

2. Nagas

On the understanding that the Federal Government of Nagaland will undertake to suspend:

a) Snipping and ambushing;
b) Imposition of Fines;
c) Kidnapping and recruiting;
d) Sabotage Activities;
e) Raiding and Firing on security posts, towns, and Administrative centres; and

f) Moving with Arms in uniform in town, villages and administrative centres and 1000 yards aways from security posts.

The understanding is confirmed that special agreement may be made in cases where movements with arms in uniform becomes necessary in any area where may be risk of encounter with security forces, eg. along or across roads or bridges.

3. The understanding given by both sides (India and Nagas) should preclude any encounter even occurring between Federal Government Personal and India Forces, the rule—"No firing unless first fire upon" will be strictly observed during the Cease fire period.

4. 7. To promote an atmosphere conducive to peaceful occupation and free discussions, the Federal Army shall not use the period of the ceasefire to Parade with Arms in inhabited areas from which the forces will not be present under this agreement .

5. 8. In the International Border areas, security forces will maintain patrolling to a depth of 3 miles as the crow flies from the frontier line. In this particular matter arangement can be made for further modification when the Ceasefire is effect.

6. 9. No arms will be imported from abroad by the Federal Government of Nagaland during the period of Ceasefire.

7. 11. The Government of India during the period of Ceasefire will continue the protection of Army Convoy on maintenance service, and the usual road patrolling, in this connection will extend to not more than 100 yards. On either side of road. The road patrols will withdraw when the convoy has passed. The Federal Army personnel shall move about freely when the convoy passed the locality and also in non-convoy days. The days of the week and

the particular routes used by convoys will be notified in advance and communicated to the Federal Government.

8. 13. The above terms applies to the Areas of Operations.

Signed on behalf of the
Federal Government of Nagaland.

1. Zashei Huire, 2. Biseto Medom, 3. L.Z. Zhenito,
10, August 1964.

Issued with the authority and
on Behalf of the Government of India.

Signed/Vishnu Sahay
14th August, 1964.

Rev. Longri Ao.
President,
Nagaland Peace Council.

Dated 15th September, 1975.

I hereby renominate and re-authorise the following persons to be Federal/NNC representatives for the talks with Indian Government.

The list of the Federal/NNC representatives is given below:

1. Maj. Gen. M. Aka.
2. Z. Ramyo.
3. Dahru.
4. Kevi Yalley.
5. Venyu Rakhiu.
6. I. Temjaba.

- The representatives hold equal Status.

Sd/-

(Zashei Huire)
President, Federal Government of Nagaland

APPENDIX V

THE PEACE MISSION'S PROPOSALS, 20 DECEMBER, 1964

1. It has been a matter of considerable satisfaction to the Peace Mission, as to all others in Nagaland and in the rest of India, that since firing ceased on 6th September, 1964, for the first time in ten years people in Nagaland are experiencing what normalcy is. The Peace Mission feels that it is the moral obligation of every one in Nagaland and more so, of the Peace Mission, in whom so much confidence and faith has been reposed, to see that peace becomes everlasting in Nagaland.
2. But first it should be placed on record to the honour of both parties that have been in conflict that the attempt to find peace and agreement to a cease-fire was an adventurous step which issued from their deep desire to find an honourable way to terminate such a bitter, wasteful and protracted conflict.
3. The marked difference in the atmosphere that prevails in Nagaland today as compared with that prevailing prior to the cessation of operation will probably be only realised by those who have lived or worked in Nagaland where there was fear as soon as darkness began and a sense of insecurity resulting from the ever present possibility of sudden violence. Today, the people are returning to their normal occupations. Families are being reunited, the biggest harvest for many years has been gathered and there is a feeling of hope in Nagaland which makes every delegate engaged in the peace talks only too conscious of the heavy burden of decision on those who have to take it, the life and happiness of so many depended on the

decisions that are taken. In all this, it is fair to pay tribute not only to the Government of India for their humanity and imagination but also to the leaders of the Baptist Church for whom this initiative was the result of much thought and powerful consideration of the good of both India and Nagaland.

4. The Nagaland Peace Talks, which started on 23 of September, 1964, have now come to a stage where the NFG delegation have placed their demands for considerations by the Government of India. This was in response to the statement of the leader of the Government of India delegation at Chedema on November 14, wherein the Government of India also stated their position and understanding of the problem, as they saw it.
5. The Nagaland Federal Delegation has claimed that the Nagas had never been conquered by the Indian Army or ruled by an Indian Government, although their territory had been forcibly annexed by the British Army and the British Government about a century ago. Nevertheless, their right of self determination, they claim, belongs to them separately as a people from the Sovereign Independent State of India, and they are now demanding recognition of this independence, which as they say, India herself demanded and heroically struggled for under the historic slogan of *Swaraj*.
6. The Government of India's position, on the other hand, is that Nagaland formed an integral part of India before 1947 and that with the transfer of power of India by the British Parliament, Nagaland became part of India in the same way as all other states in India. At the same time the Government of India claim that they have already accepted the need for granting the fullest autonomy to Nagaland by constituting the State of Nagaland so as to ensure the fullest development of the Nagas and to guarantee their separate ethnic and cultural entity and to ensure their traditional right and their resources. Accordingly, the Nagas are not ruled by the alien power but are ruling themselves.
7. The Peace Mission notes that a section of the Naga people accepted the status of Statehood thus conferred upon

Nagaland as being in their best interest. Another section did not consider that it satisfied the aims and objectives they had been fighting for. Thus there are theses two divergent positions of the Government of India and the NFG confronting each other.

8. Though the two positions appear to be far apart, the Peace Mission believes that, with goodwill and understanding on both sides, a solution acceptable to both can be found.
9. As earlier stated, the Peace Mission reiterates that it is under an inescapable moral obligation to ensure maintenance of peace and settlement of all outstanding problems through peaceful means. The Peace Mission believes that there is human problem that cannot be solved by peaceful means. The Peace Mission further believes that the Government's concerned and the people concerned share and subscribe to this view.
10. While the Peace Mission fully agrees and endorses the principle that all subject peoples have the right of self determination and that no group of people is competent to rule over another, it also has to invite the attention of the Nagaland Federal Government to certain historical processes that had taken place to give birth to the Union of India and to the emergence of the great concepts and ideals underlying the Union Constitution.
11. The British had conqured at several stages and in diverse manner, various parts of the India sub-continent, comprising different ethnic groups, political systems and religions. However, under the aegis of the Indian National Congress and since 1920, under the leadership of Mahatma Gandhi, these various different peoples, representing diverse linguistic, cultural, ethnic and religious elements, came together against foreign colonial rule and developed a consciousness of nationhood. Unfortunately, this common struggle against foreign imperialism, that had welded these diverse peoples in the Indian sub-continent into one nation, did not somehow have an appreciable impact on the Nagas. This was, no doubt, due to the policy of isolation and exclusion, so deftly practised by British rulers, who believed in creating pockets contrary to each other and hoping to rule in perpetuity by dividing the peoples.

In any case, this great national movement of unification which freed India including Nagaland from the yoke of foreign rule did not bring within its embracing sweep the Naga population to the same extent as it did in the other parts of the sub-continent. Thus, in 1947, when all the diverse people of India, who had been brought under British rule, voluntarily agreed to form the Union of India and to share in the common endeavour to ensure that in this great Union the ideals of Fraternity, Liberty, Justice and Equality, as enshrined in the Constitution, are fully achieved for a common benefit of all, the same response and sense of participation was not noticeable in the Naga areas.

12. The Peace Mission, in the circumstances, appreciates and understands the desire of the Nagas for self-determination and their urge to preserve their integrity. The Peace Mission also appreciates the courage and tenacity, displayed by the Naga people in their endeavour to achieve this goal. The objectives which they have placed before themselves in their memorandum "Naga Peace Declaration" dated 11, December, 1964, and addressed to the Peace Mission, namely, their desire to find peace, their resolve to maintain their integrity and to resist entanglement in war, are all extremely laudable and should command themselves to all peace loving people. It is, however, to be noted that this Declaration, in itself, does not resolve the political issue. Therefore, some appropriate meeting point has to be found, where the aims and ideals of the NFG can be achieved, at the same time, making it possible for the Government of India to accept these within the framework of the political settlement to be mutually agreed upon.

13. The Peace Mission in the pursuit of a settlement through peaceful means, to which the Government of India as well as the NFG equally subscribe, would like both the Government of India and the NFG to consider seriously whether such a meeting point could be reached. On the one hand, the NFG could, on their own volition, decide to be a participant in the Union of India and mutually settle the terms and conditions for that purpose. On the other

hand, the Government of India could consider to what extent the pattern and structure of the relationship between the Nagaland and the Government of India should be adapted and recast, so as to satisfy the political aspirations of all sections of Naga opinion and to make it possible for the ideals of peace as expressed in the Naga Peace Declaration to be substantially realised.

14. The Peace Mission would like, in all earnestness, to impress upon both sides that the approach, herein suggested, is not only the fairest, but the only practical one in the given circumstance; and it fervently hopes that it will command itself to the Government of India as well as to the Nagaland Federal Government.

15. The Peace Mission reiterates that the peace now obtaining in Nagaland should be made everlasting. With that object in view, the Peace Mission offered certain suggestions, whereupon both the parties had unequivocally affirmed and declared that they would renounce war and violence as a means for political settlement. This declaration of renunciation of war and use of armed force, it is earnestly emphasised, must not be deviated from by any menas. The Peace Mission's proposal, following this bilateral declaration of renunciation of war, to deposit all underground arms in safe custody and to withdraw all Indian security force from law and order duties could not unfortunately be implemented.

16. Nevertheless, the Peace Mission would earnestly desire that, in faithful pursuance of the Declaration of renunciation of use of armed forces, both parties take concrete steps to remove all frictions. There have been numerous complaints and counter-complaints from both. The Peace Mission would suggest that the NFG require all arms issued to its forces to be concentrated at one or several places, in their armouries and under their custody, so that there can be no basis for any future complaint of their forces parading with arms or extorting money or supplies under threat. They should also seriously ask themselves whether further recruiting and movement out of Nagaland towards Pakistan does not create an impression that these are only acts preparatory to resumption of hostilities and,

if so, they should take remedial measures by putting a step to such recruitment and movement. The Government of India should ensure that its security forces and the civil administration continue to abide strictly with the terms of the agreement, both in spirit and letter.

17. The Peace Mission makes a fervent appeal for consideration of the suggestions contained in this paper and for all actions that is possible for the maintenance of peace.

20.12.1964

Bimalprasad Chaliha
Jayaprakash Narayan and
Michael Scott.

APPENDIX VI

SHILLONG ACCORD

The Shillong Accord of 11 November 1975 Between the Government of India and the Underground Nagas

1. The following representatives of the underground organisation met the Governor of Nagaland Shri L.P. Singh, representing the Government of India, at Shillong on 10 and 11, November 1975.

    1. Shri I. Temjenba
    2. Shri S. Dahru
    3. Shri Venyiyi Rhakhu
    4. Shri Z. Ramyo
    5. Shri M. Assa
    6. Shri Kevi Yallay

2. There were series of four discussions. Some of the discussions were held with the Governor alone; at other, the Governor was assisted by the two Advisers for Nagaland, Shri. Ramunny and Shri H. Zopianga, and Shri M.B. Kampani, Joint Secretary in the Ministry of Home Affairs. All the five members of the Liaison Committee namely Rev. Longri Ao. Dr. M. Aram, Shri L. Lungalang, Shri Kenneth Kerhuo and Shri Lungshim Shaiza, participated in the discussions.
3. The following were the outcome of the discussions:

    i) Representatives of the underground organisations conveyed their decision, of their own volition, to accept, without condition, the Constitution of India.

ii) It was agreed that the arms, now underground, would be brought out and deposited at appointed places. Details for giving effect to this agreement will be worked out between them and representatives of the Government, the security forces, and members of the Liaison Committee;

iii) It was agreed that the representatives of the underground organisations should have reasonable time to formulate other issues for discussion for final settelment.

Dated, Shillong, 11 November, 1975

I. Temjenba, S. Dahru
Z. Ramyo, Ma. Assa
Kevi Yallay, L.P. Singh

On behalf of the representatives
On behalf of the Government of India.
On underground organisations.

Supplementary Agreement to the Shillong Accord on 5 January, 1976

Implementation of Clause II of Shillong Accord of 11 November 1975.

1. It was decided that the collection of arms initially at collection centres, would commence as early as possible, and will be completed by 25 January 1976. Initial places of collection to be decided through discussion between Commissioner, representatives of underground organisations and the members of the Liaison Committee.
2. Once all arms are collected, these will be handed over to the Peace Council team at the respective places of collections.
3. Peace Council team will arrange to transport the arms

from collection centres to Chedema Peace Camp and arrange guards etc. for safe custody of arms.

4. Similar arrangement at agreed place/places will be made in Manipur with concerrence with the Manipur Government.
5. The underground may stay at Peace Camp to be established at suitable places, and their maintenance will be arranged by the Peace Council. Any voluntary contributions from and sources will be made to the Peace Council, who will utilise the fund according to necessity.

Beseto Medom Keyho
Pukrove Nakro
Z. Ramyo
I. Temjenba

L.P. Singh
Governor

Dated Shillong, 5 January, 1976.

APPENDIX VII

DESAI-PHIZO TALK, 14.6.1977, LONDON

DESAI : What happened to your face?
PHIZO : It's paralysis.
DESAI : When it happened ?
PHIZO : In 1942.
DESAI : So many years ago ?
PHIZO : Yes.
DESAI : How it come about?
PHIZO : I was a war prisoner.
DESAI : Then this happened from prison?
PHIZO : Yes, I have come to meet the Prime Minister of India and I have been waiting for an oppurtunity like this one for a long time and I could meet you today.
DESAI : Aram told me that you wanted to see me alone .
PHIZO : No, I did not say that .
DESAI : Have you met Aram?
PHIZO : No. I have not met him and I do not know him. I have come to meet the Prime minister of India because of my people have been suffering for a very long time. As you have become the Prime Minister of India for only about three months and I am not blaming you for our sufferings, that I want you to understand but I thought we could find a way out to bring an end on the matter.
DESAI : The Nagas are not suffering and if you talk about Nagaland I shall not talk with you. I told your neice Rano that I am prepared to meet you as a person but not about Nagaland.
PHIZO : In 1947, when the British were about to leave their empire, a Naga delegation went to Delhi tc meet

Mahatma Gandhi because our situation may not have been understood by the Indians. And we explained to Mahatma Gandhi that the Nagas are not Indians and Nagaland is not Indian territory. We submitted the points of discussion to Mahatma Gandhi earlier as his secretary asked us to do. I think his secretary was Pyarelal. We asked Gandhi if Indians will attack Nagaland if it became free. Gandhi said, if you say that Nagas are not Indians and Nagaland is not Indian territory then the matter must stop there. We also do not want to the British and the matter must stop there. India will not attack you. She has no right to do so and I will sacrifice my life for you before any Naga is shot.

DESAI : From where the meeting took place?

PHIZO : In Delhi at Bhangi Colony. Mahatma Gandhi was assassinated so soon. If he had lived a few months longer the Naga problem would not have arisen, but if we do what Mahatma Gandhi would have said were there will be no difficulty.

DESAI : Why have you brought up Gandhi's name? I know him better than you. I will not follow him. I will do everything what I consider to be right. Now, what more do you want to say ?

PHIZO : I have come to meet the Prime Minister of India because the Nagas have been suffering for a very long time and we must find a way to end the trouble.

DESAI : I have told you that the Nagas are not suffering. I know everything. And therefore there is nothing to discuss. Nagaland became a State of India in 1960, before that it was Assam.

PHIZO : How Nagaland could become a state of India?

DESAI : It was the Nagas who came and asked for a state and it was given to them.

PHIZO : But that is an argument and I don't come here to argue with you. The Government of India may claim something on their part and the Nagas upheld some thing on their part and there may be a wide gap between us. But the problem is more serious than the argument and I wish that we could find a way and go into the matter more deeply.

DESAI : No, I will not talk about Nagaland. And If you want to talk about Nagaland this is the end of the meeting.

PHIZO : I am already 73, and you are older than me. How long are we going to be here? Even if you and I do not agree today that is not the end, so we must find a way to solve our problem. And the sooner the better. Are you not as good as the British who gave freedom to India?

DESAI : Why you talk of the British now? Who are they ? It is said the Aryans came to India and all that; but what is the use of talking about the past ? We are already here and what else. You are a foreigner. You are staying in a foreign country. You receive reports and talk about it. I have all the reports and there is no problem. I know everything. I am the Prime minister of India. Nobody needs to tell me that there is a problem.

PHIZO : We the people of Asia fought against the white imperialists and how could we Asians fight and kill each other?

DESAI : Why bringing up Asia, it is India.

PHIZO : Will the Prime Minister of India exterminate all the Nagas ?

DESAI : Yes, I will exterminate all the Naga rebels. There will be no mercy.

PHIZO : Is not that horrible?

DESAI : We are protecting our citizens. Only a few Nagas are giving trouble, harassing the people in the villages, that we cannot allow. We must protect our citizens. And I will exterminate all. There will be no mercy.

PHIZO : Whether we are few of many I thought we could go into the matter deeper.

DESAI : I told you that I shall not discuss about Nagaland and if you want to talk about Nagaland this is the end of the meeting. What more do you want to say?

PHIZO : Well, my meeting you today as it is, is more in the nature of making an acquaintance with you. As our case is a long standing one which we could not decide it in a day. I have some Naga colleagues with me including my daughter and my son. I want them to come and meet you and hear from you what you have said to me. Can I go and bring them in?

DESAI : Yes.

PHIZO : I have told the Prime Minister of India that the Nagas are suffering terribly for so many years.

DESAI : The Nagas are suffering because they are persisting on Independence. You and all who are outside are welcome back to become Indians. But, if you want to talk only about Naga independence, I wont talk to you.

KHODAO: When you are elected Prime Minister, because all through your life you fought, Nagas thought you will be the man for final settlement of the Naga problem.

DESAI : What is to settle ? I will have absolutely no leniency on rebels. If you want to persist on Independence I will have nothing to talk. I will certainly exterminate the rebel Nagas. I have no compunction in that.

PHIZO : Mr. Prime Minister, will there be further oppurtunity for discussion?

DESAI : What discussion. There will be no discussion.

APPENDIX VIII

THE SPEECH OF MR. ISAK CHISHI SWU, Chairman National Socialist Council of Nagaland at Geneva UN Conference on Indigenous Peoples on 27th July, 1993

Highly respected Medamo Chairperson,. distinguished representatives and the honourable members of the congregation.

This is the first time for the Nagas to be privileged with such exalted platform of freedom. I am exceedingly delighted to seize this occasion to introduce ourselves as a distinct people and nation to this August congregation of different nations and peoples of the world. For a nation like our's, being choked up without any outlet to the outside world, this would also mean the finest of opportunities to enable us to speak out against the flagrant violation of our inalienable right of self-existence and subjection of our people to untold bitter state of affairs for the past 40 years on account of preposterous occupation of our homeland by the Indian and Burmese armed forces.

Allow me first of all, to express on behalf of my people, the immense urge we have for the cause of the world's indigenous people though our case may be different. The helpless indigenous millions are now driven to the point that borders total extinction. It has become the greatest challenge for the world to be concerned about the salvation of the downtrodden if justice is at all for every people. It is too long a time to keep the rights and due shares of the weak and the indigenous people deprived of. Where is peace if justice is not donned? This is the failure of the world today and it simply cannot be allowed to go at this rate. Rectification is a must if it to exist for humanity, for to promise a future is the sacred obligation of the world to itself. This responsibility falls upon the United Nations so long as it claims to represent the world. This must be fulfilled and to this end our Naga people shall remain committed.

Permit me to say about my country. We come from free Nagaland. It is situated in between China, India and Burma. We are of distinct Mongoloid race who migrated to this present Naga inhabited compact areas from the east, a few thousand years ago. We are the first settlers of the land. Our population is about 3 millions. The size of the Naga inhabited area is approximately 100,000 sq. km.

Naga have their history and it does not admit of any attempts at distortion. Nagas as a distinct nation remain unconquered, unadministered and independent from time immemorial though this reality is hardly known to the outside world. Only a small portion of its territory entered the recorded history of the British imperialism in 1838 when some Naga villages were invaded by the British forces. This years also marks the beginning of their war of resistance against the political campaigns and military occupations, division and destruction of their land and institution by the invading forces. The British imperialist left India and their occupied Nagaland on the 15th August, 1947. The Nagas under the British occupation promptly declared their independence on the 14, August, 1947 one day ahead of India and it was informed to the United Nations. Thereafter it was merged with the unconquered and unadministered 'Free Nagaland'. It was confirmed by the plebiscite of 1951 where 99.9 voted in favour of Sovereign Independence. India refused to recognise it. Negotiations went on and arrived at "The Nine-Points Agreement" on the 27–30 June, 1947. But within a few weeks of signing the agreement India abrogated it unilaterally. Yet peaceful approach continued from the Nagas fully believing in the declared lofty "non-violence principle" till 1954. But India deliberately despised and launched unscrupulous massive invasion on Nagaland with the sole view to exterminating the Nagas and their nation at the earliest opportunity. Since then fierce fighting started and continues till today. Thus the Indo-Naga issue is neither a question of 'separation' nor 'secessions' from India. But is is a war of resistance against invasion. Because separation or secessions comes only when there is a union. Nagaland was and is never a part of India nor that a Burma either by conquest or by consent. And as such ours is a case of resistance against the invasion of Nagaland by India and Burma and a case of recognition of the inalienable right of self-existence of the Naga people.

Destruction and suffering inflicted upon the Nagas in the past forty years are beyond description. Losses in terms of life and property are immeasurable—thousands were indiscriminately killed, thousands tortured to death, thousands died of starvation and diseases in concentration camps and jails. Raping of women were daily phenomena. Burning down of villages, destruction of crops were time and again carried out of all which outside world know virtually nothing. In our recorded history there are about 1.5 lakh killed. What is more, unlike others, Nagaland is sandwiched between two hostile nationa—India in the west and Burma in the east. Helpless innocent public are choked up without outlet to the outside world. All happenings are kept sealed off. Only reporters who served the interest of the adversary are permitted except Gavin Young (London Observer) whose publication was banned by the Indian Government. We are greatly grateful to the Human Right Organisation People for their undaunted struggle for the cause of humanity things might have taken the worst course. Violations of human rights have been countless and nonstop. There is the horror of Indian and Burmese State terrorism in Nagaland. But it must be made known clearly that in spite of such genocide of population Nagas have not retaliated against any civilian of Burma and India. Believe it or not, there is not a single case of an innocent Indian or Burmese having been killed. Even the Indian Armymen who fell into the Nagas' hand were treated well. Thus, around 240 Indian armed personnel including 9 air crew captured by the Naga Army were treated with dignity and released on humanitarian grounds. Are all these signs of being terrorists as Indians maliciously termed? Absolutely not. It is wise to maintain a standard of ethics. The whole world knows how India and Burma behave notwithstanding their exalted claim in moral philosophy. Our forbearance should not be misconstructed to mean as a sign of weakness. There is limit to tolerance and it is simply no good to wait for reprisal, for forty years of patience is enough.

Nagas have been invariably confronted with the real war of massive military operations, massive political suppressions, massive economic exploitation and the endless assimilation processes. Ceaseless influx of alien people has reached alarming proportion. Our land are grabbed from all sides, mineral resources exploited. Forests are cut down solely for selfish ends. Most of the countrysides are left barren. Ruthless exploitation in the past decades by the colonial agents has dangerously tilted the ecological balance of our beautiful richly gifted land.

The desire of the strong to dominate the weak persists everywhere, seeking pretext of various kinds through arbitrary legislation to justify the use of force. This has been the reality and it has provoked irreconcilable problems terribly victimising the weak and the indigenous in the name of the so-called sustainability and modern civilisation. We think the brunt we bore over the years for this real challenge of extermination merits the attention of the congregation. We do think the ordeals we have been withstanding to save ourselves from the danger of extermination deserve sympathy support. If exploitation in any form in all fields shall not be halted no individual indigenous people would ever be saved from the eventuality of total extinction. It is a crucial challenge. It must be met. We, therefore, urge that the right of the weak people and the indigenous to self-determination be safeguarded at all costs. Without this birthright being securely in their hands they have absolutely nothing. We are inspired beyond words to see that the Asia Indigenous People Pact has been founded to uphold the legitimate cause of the downtrodden million indigenous. The world organisation should in no case lag behind in this issue.

Many thanks

Bibliography

PRIMARY SOURCES

OFFICIAL DOCUMENTS

Government of India

Parliamentary Debates on Naga Issues, Government Reports:

Lok Sabha Debates: Starred question. Vol. V. Tenth Session, 22 August to 16 September, 1955.

——; Starred question, Vol. II, Eleventh Session, 21 November to 23 December 1955.

——: On Situation in Nagas Hills, Vol. III, Part I. 17 Arpil to 14 May, 1956.

——: Rebel Naga, Vol. IV, Part I, 15 May to 30 May, 1956.

——: Situation in Naga Hills, Vol. VI, Part II, 16 July to 3 August, 1956.

——: Nehru Statement, North-East Frontier Agency, Vol. VI, Part II, 16 August to 3 September, 1955.

——: Nehru Statement on Situation on Naga Hills, Vol. VII, Part II, 6 August to 25 August, 1956.

——: Vol. VIII, Part I, 14 November to 11 December 1956.

——: Naga Hills Tuensang Area Bill, Second Series, Vol. IX, 25 November to 6 December, 1957.

——: Vol. XLIV, Second Series, 1 to 12 August, 1960.

——: Nehru Statement, Anti Indian propaganda by Mr. Phizo in UK Vol. XLIV, Second Series 1 to 12 August, 1960.

——: Report entry of Naga Hostile to Nagalnd, Vol. XXX, Third Series, 15–28 April, 1964.
——: Out come of Prime Minister Talks with Underground Naga Delegation, Vol. LXI, Sixteenth Series, 16 to 30 November, 1966.
——: Report Celebration of Republic Day by the so called Nagaland Federal Government, (Dinesh Singh statement) Vol. LII, Third Series, 16 to 29 March, 1966.
Rajya Sabha Debates; Underground Naga Leaders views on Naga issue, Vol. LVIII, Nos. 1–8, 7 to 17 November, 1966, Rajya Sabha Secretariat, New Delhi.
Parliamentary Debates: *Trans-bordered Disputes between India and Burma,* Vol. II, Part I, 9 July to 11 August, 1952.
Parliamentary Debates; Statement Re Prime Minister talks with the underground Naga delegation (Dinesh Singh), Vol. LVIII, 7 to 17 November, 1966.

State Government

Bareh, H.C. 1970, Gazetteers of India, Nagaland Distirct Gazetteers Unit, Kohima, Nagaland, 1970..
Nagaland: Island of Peace, Directorate of Information and Publicity, Kohima, Nagaland.
Nagaland (1990), Directorate of Information and Publicity, Government of Nagaland, Kohima.
Nagas' 90 All Things Become New (1990) Published by Literature Committees 90 Nagas', Kohima Nagaland.

Documents Reports and Correspondence Letters

A Brief Political Account, NSCN, 1993. (Unpublished)
Annual Administration Report of the Naga Hills Political Agency, Calcutta Foreign Department Press, 1876–1877.
Bilateral Agreement on Ceasefire 1964
Bower, Ursula Graham; *The Naga Problem,* 1967. (Unpublished)
Brief Notes on the Naga Hills District (Burma) with details of routes (Simla, 1942). Burma Defence Department.
Connor, Mitchell; Report on a tour in the Naga Hills District (Burma) season December 1939 to April 1940 (Rangoon, 1940).

Emergence of Naga National Council, 1946.

Geneva Documents (Oral statement delivered by Mr. Isak Chishi on the 16th Evening Session, 1995, accredited society for threatened peoples on February, 7–9, 1995 (Geneva) 51st session of the United Nations Commission on Human Rights. (Agenda Item 10.)

General Mowu's Presentation of Naga Case to U.S.A. in July, 1986.

Indian General Staff Military Report on the Naga Hills including routes (Simla, 1914)-N.B. This Report is also found in the India Office Records. Ref L/MIL/17/18/23. L/Ps/20/D201.

Letter to Rajiv Gandhi, Prime Minister, Republic of India, 7 August, 1985.

Naga Hills, District of the Annual Administration Report of the Naga Hills Political Agency for 1875–76.

Maitland, Pelham James; *Detailed Report on the Naga Hills Expedition of 1879–80* (Simla, 1880).

Naga Club Diamond Jubilee (1918–1993), 7 January, 1993.

Naga Nation Struggle Against Genocide, Publication IWGIA, Netherland, 1986.

Naga Voluntary Plebiscite, Naga National Council Kohima, Nagaland, 16 May, 1951.

Naga National Rights & Movement, NNC, 1993. (Unpublished)

New Facts of Nagaland Boundary, 4 March, 1979.

Pawsey, Sir Charles; *The Naga Problem*, Confidential Paper, 1965.

Phizo, A.Z.; A profile: Prepared by Dr. Visier Sanyu on behalf of Organising Committee for the Funeral of Dr. A.Z. Phizo.

Phizo, A.Z; *The Fate of the Naga People* Publication, NNC, 1960. (Unpublished)

Phizo, A.Z.; *Design for Genocide*, Unpublished, 1960.

Phizo letter to C. Rajagopalachari. Presidency Jail, Calcutta, 22 November, 1948 .

Phizo letter to Rajiv Gandhi, 10 May, 1986.

Phizo's Letter to the President of Republic of India, 1 January, 1951.

Phizo's letter to Mr. Jeffery Evans. Arizona, U.S.A, 5 April, 1982.

Phizo's Letter to President of U.N.O. 8 October, 1960.

Report of the Administration of the District of the Naga Hills, Calcutta Foreign Department Press, 1878–1885.

Report on the Administration of the District of the Naga Hills, 1876–79, Simla, Calcutta.

Report on the Tours in the Naga Hills from 8th January–7th April, 1940 (Rangoon, 1940).

Scott, M.; *The Nagas. India's problem—or the world's?* 1967.

Selection of Papers Regarding the Hill Tracts between Assam and Burma and on the Upper Brahmaputra, Calcutta (1873).

Shillong Accord. 10 & 11, Nov. 1975.

Sixteen Point Agreement, July 1960.

Sumi, Huska; The Naga Nationalism Movement, Seminar Paper, Sumi Kiphemi Kukhakalu Golden Jubillee, 17 January, 1996.

Supplementary Agreement to the Shillong Accord, 5 January, 1976.

The Hydari Agreement, June 1947.

The Naga Nation and its Struggle Against Genocide, Publication, *IWGIA*, 1968. (Document)

The Naga Problem, External Publicity Division: Ministry of External Affairs Government of India: New Delhi, 1962.

The National Rights and Movement, NNC (Unpublished), 1993.

Where Peacekeepers Have Declared War, Publication, NCCAMRAFA, Delhi, 1997.

Year Book of the United Nations, 1960 (New York), Columbia University Press, 1961, p. 48.

Year Book of the United Nations, Vol. 46, Department of Public Information. UN, New York, Matinus Nijhoff Publishers, 1992, pp. 326–394.

SECONDARY SOURCES

Books

Aitchison, C.U.; (Compiled): A Collection of Treaties Engagements and Sanads, Relating to India and Neighbouring Countries (Revised and Continued upto 1929) Vol. XII, Mittal Publication, New Delhi, 1983 (Reprinted).

Alemchiba, M.; *A Brief Historical Account of Nagaland.* The Naga Institute of Culture, Kohima, Nagaland, 1970.

Anand, V.K.; *Conflict in Nagland,* Chanakya Publication, New Delhi, 1980.

Anand, V.K.; *Nagaland in Transition,* Associated Publishing House, New Delhi, 1967.

Anderson, Benedict; (Reprinted) "Imagined Communities, (Reflection on the Origin and Spread of Nationalism) revise edition, Verso Publication, London, New York, 1994.

Ao, Tajenyuba; *British occupation of Naga country,* Published by Naga Literature Society, Nagaland.

Aram, M.; *Peace in Nagaland. Eight Years Story* (1964–74) Arnold Heinemann Publications, New Delhi, 1974.

Bendangangshi; *Glimpses of Naga History,* Published by Naga Patriots from Soyim, Mokokchung, Nagaland, 1993.

Brass, Paul R.; *Ethnicity and Nationalism. Theory and Comparison,* Sage Publication, New Delhi, 1991.

Brown, David; *The State and Ethnic Politics in South East Asia,* Routledge, London, 1994.

Burton, John and Dukes, Frank; *Conflict: Practice and Management Settlement and Resolution,* St. Martin's Press, New York, 1990.

Campbell, Arthur; *The Siege from Kohima,* London, 1956.

Captain, Michell St. John F.; *The North-East Frontier of India,* (A topographical, Political and Military Report) Vikas Publishing House, Delhi, 1973.

Chatterjee, R.K.; *India's Land Borders,* Sterling Publication, 1978.

Clow, Andrew; *Future Administration of Assam Tribal People,* Shillong, 1945.

Coupland, Sir Reginald; *The Indian Problem: Report on the Constitutional Problem in India,* London, 1944.

Crane, Robert; *Role of Ethnic Nationalism,* Hudson Inst., 1967.

Danda, A.K.; *Ethnicity in India,* Inter India Publication, New Delhi, 1991.

De Silva, K.M. and Mayeds, R.J.; *Internationalisation of Ethnic Conflict,* Pinter, London, 1991.

Elwin, Verrier; *Nagaland,* (P. Dutta for the Research Department Adviser's Secretariat), Shillong, 1961.

——: *The Nagas in the Nineteenth Century,* Oxford University Press, 1969.

Engineer, Asghar Ali; *Ethnic Conflict in South Asia,* Ajanta Publication, Delhi, 1987.

Gavin, Young; *The Naga: An Unknown War,* London, 1962.

Ghosh, B.B.; *History of Nagaland,* Chand Publication, 1982.

Ghosh, P.S.; *Co-operation and Conflict in South Asia,* Manohar Publication, New Delhi, 1989.

Grierson, G.; *Linguistic Survey of India,* Vol. III, Part II + III, Tibeto Burman Family, Calcutta, 1847.

Gundevia, Y.D.; *War and Peace in Nagaland,* Palit & Palit Publishers, New Delhi, 1975.

Gunther, Bacher (ed.); *Federalism Against Ethnicity,* International Legal and Democratic Institute to Prevent Minority Conflicts, Rugger Verlag Publication, 1997.

Gurr, Ted Robert and Hariff Barbara; *Ethnic Conflict in World Politics,* West View Press, Boulder San Francisco, 1993.

Haimendorf, Christian Von Furer; *Nagaland Revisited,* Geographical Publication, 1971.

——: *Return to the Naked Nagas,* 1976 John Murray reprint of Methuen Publication, 1939.

——: *Naked Nagas,* London, 1939.

Hasler, Martin (ed.); *Ethnic Conflict in the World,* American Academy of Political and Social Science, Philadelphia, The Academy, 1987.

Hazarika, S.; *Stranger of the Mist,* (Rev. Ed.) Penguin Books Published, 1995.

Hecter, Michael; *Internal Colonialism: The celtic Fringe in British National Development,* London: Routledge and Kegan Paul, 1975.

Hobsbawm, E.J.; (Reprinted) *Nations and Nationalism since 1780,* Cambridge University Press, Cambridge, 1991.

Hodson T.C.; *The Naga Tribes of Manipur,* Macmillan, London, 1911.

Horam, Dr. M.; *North-East India, A Profile,* Cosmo Publication, New Delhi, 1990.

——: *Naga Polity* (Reprinted) Low Price Publications, Delhi, 1992.

——: *Naga Insurgency,* Cosmo Publications, Delhi, 1988.

Horpwitz, Donald L.; *Ethnic Groups in Conflict,* Barkeley, California, University of California Press, 1985.

Hutnik, Nimmi; *Ethnic Minority Identity: A Social Psychological Perspective,* Clarendon Press, Oxford, 1991.

Hutton, J.H.; *Angami Nagas,* Oxford University Press, London, (Reprinted by Government of Nagaland), 1969.

Hutton, J.H.; *The Sema Nagas,* Oxford University Press, London, (Reprinted by Government of Nagaland), 1967.

Jacob, Julian.; *The Nagas: Hill People of North-East India,* Publication, 1990.

Johnson, J.; *My Experiences in Manipur and the Naga Hills,* Reprinted Delhi, 1971.

——: *Manipur and Naga Hills,* Vivek Publishing House, Delhi (Reprinted), 1971.

Kellas, James G.; *The Politics of Nationalism and Ethnicity,* Macmillan Publication, London, 1991.

Kumar, B.B.; *Tension and Conflict in North-East India,* Cosmo Publications, New Delhi, 1995.

Lawandowski, S.; *Migration and Ethnicity in India,* Manohar Publications, New Delhi, 1980.

Lintner, Bertil.; *Land of Jade: A Journey Through Insurgent Burma,* Kiscadale Publication, Bangkok, 1990.

Luithui, L. & N.; Haksar, (1984) *Nagaland File: A Question of Human Rights,* Lancer International, New Delhi.

Mackenzie, A.; *History of the Relations of Government with Hill Tribes of the North-East Frontier of Bengal,* Calcutta, Government of Bengal, 1884.

Mackenzie, A.; *The North-East Frontier of India,* Mittal Publications, New Delhi, 1979.

Mankekar, D.R.; *On the Slippery Slope in Nagaland,* Bombay, 1967.

Mathew, Jack; *A Story of the Naga Hills, (illustrated)* G. Bell 7 Sons; London, 1941.

Maxwell, Neville; *India: The Nagas & The North-East,* Report No. 17. Revised Edition, Minority Right group, 1980.

Mills, J.P.; *The Ao Nagas,* Oxford University Press, Bombay (Reprinted by Government of Nagaland), 1973.

——: *The Lotha Nagas,* Oxford University Press, Bombay (Reprinted by Government of Nagaland), 1973.

——: *The Rengma Nagas,* Oxford University Press, Bombay (Reprinted by Government of Nagaland), 1973.

Mishra, Udayan; *North-East India, Quest for Identity,* (The Naga National Question) Omsons publication, Guwahati, 1988, pp. 1–54.

Moyniham, Daniel Patrick; *Pandemonium, Ethnicity in International Politics.* Oxford University Press, 1993.

Mullik, B.N.; *My Years with Nehru,* 1948–64, Delhi, Allied Publishers, 1972.

Nari, R.; *Enchanted Frontiers,* Oxford University Press, 1971.

Neville, M.; *India's China War,* Pelican Book, 1972.

Nibedon, Nirmal, *North-East India—The Night of the Guerrillas,* Lancers Publishers, New Delhi, 1978.

Nibedon, Nirmal; *North-East India: The Ethnic Explosion,* Lancers Publishers, New Delhi, 1981.

Nuh, V.K.; *Efforts Toward Naga Unity,* Publication, CNBC, 1993.

——: *Episode of the Naga Tragedy,* Publication, Vision 1995.

——: *Nagaland Church and Politics,* Publication, 1986.

Pakem, B. (ed.); *Nationality, Ethnicity and Cultural Identity. Regionalism in India: North-East,* Omsons Publications, Guwahati, 1990.

Phadnis, Urmila; *Ethnicity and Nation-Building in South Asia,* Sage Publications, New Delhi, 1990.

Pruitt, Dean; *Negotiation Behaviour,* New York: Academic Press, 1981.

Rammuny, M.; *The World of Nagas,* Northern Books Centre, New Delhi, 1988.

Reid, Sir Robert; *History of the Frontier Areas Bordering on Assam,* Eastern Publication House, Delhi, 1983.

Rivenburg, N.; *The Star of the Naga Hills,* Philadelphia, 1941.

Rothschild, Joseph; *Ethnic Politics: Conceptual Framework,* New York, Columbia University Press, 1981.

Ryan, Stephen; *Ethnic Conflict and International Relations,* Aldersont, Pontmonth, 1990.

Said, Abdul A., and Simmons, Duis (ed.); Ethnicity in an International Context. The Politics of Dissociation, New Brumswick, New Jersey Transaction Books, 1976.

Sareen, H.K.; *Insurgency in North-East India,* (A Study of Sino American Role), Sterling Publishers Pvt. Ltd. New Delhi, 1980.

Sarin, V.K.; *India's Northeast in Flames,* Vikas Publishing House, Ltd, New Delhi, 1982.

Scott, M.; *The Nagas: The Search for Peace,* 1966.

Shakespear, L.W.; *History of Upper Assam, Burma and North-Eastern Frontier,* London, 1914.

Shields, Federick L.; (ed.) *Ethnic Separatism and World Politics.* Lauham M.D.; University Press of America, 1984.

Sills, David L. (ed.); *Nationalism, International Encyclopaedia of the Social Sciences.* The Macmillan Company and the Free Press, Vol. 11, 1968, pp. 63–69.

——: *Ethnic Groups: International Encyclopaedia of the Social Science,* the Macmillan company and the Free press, Vol. V, 1968, pp. 167–172.

Singh, K.S; *Ethnicity, Identity and Development.* New Delhi, Manohar Publications, 1990.

——: *Tribal Movements in India,* Vol. I, Manohar Publications, New Delhi, 1982.

Singh Prakash; *Nagaland,* Publication; National Book Trust 1972.

Slim, Sir William, Field Marshall; *Defeat into Victory,* London, 1956.

Smith, Martin; *Burma,* Zed Books Publication, 1991.

Smith, Anthony D.; (Reprinted) *The Ethnic origins of Nations,* Basil Blackwell Ltd., Oxford, 1989.

——: *The Ethnic Revival,* Cambridge University Press, London, 1981.

——: *Nationalist Movements,* Macmillan Press Ltd. London, 1976.

Smith, W.C.; *The Ao Naga Tribes of Assam,* London, 1925.

Stavenhagen, Roddofo; *The Ethnic Question. Conflict, Development and Human Right,* United Nations University Press, 1990.

Stevenson, H.N.C.; *The Hill People of Burma,* London, 1944.

Stracey, P.D. *Nagaland Nightmare,* Allied Publishers, Bomaby, 1968.

Suhrke, Astri and Noble, Garner Lela; (ed.) *Ethnic Conflict in International Relations,* New York, Praeger, 1977.

Swinson, Arthur; *Kohima,* Cassell Publication London, 1966.

Ursula, Graham Bower; *Hidden Land,* John Murray Publication, 1953.

Ursula, Graham Bower; *Naga Path,* John Murray Publication, 1950. (Unpublished)

Verghese, B.G.; *India's Northeast Resurgent: Ethnicity, Insurgency, Governance, Development,* Konark Publisher, 1995.

Ward, David; *Nagaland: The Tears Behind the Blindfold*, Manuscript NCHRG, 1997.

Wati, L.; *Fact and Growth of Naga Nationalism, (Mimeographed)* 1993.

Yonou, A.; *The Rising Nagas*, Vivek Publishing House, New Delhi, 1979.

ARTICLES

Journals/Magazines/ Newspapers

Achong, P. Joseph; Dimthan. "Crisis of Manipur Integrity", *Nagaland Post*, 9 September, 1997.

Ahmed, Samina; "The Politics of Ethnicity in India", Regional Study, Vol. XI, No. 9, Autumn 1991, pp. 22–51.

Aier, L.; "The Naga Situation an Analysis", *Nagaland Post*, 7 March 1997.

——: "The Naga Situation an Analysis", *Nagaland Post*, 7 March, 1997.

Ward, David; *Kuknalim Without a Single Rifle Shot*, Nagaland Post, 16 April, 1996.

Army claims to have silenced rebel guns in North-East, *The Telegraph*, 24 October, 1996.

Arzpe, Lourdes; "Ethnicity, Nations and Culture", *Development*, No. 4, 1993, pp. 6–8.

Atlanta peace meet: "Talks on with Naga rebels at parallel summit." 4 August, *The Statesman*, 1997.

Axell Karin & Wallensteen; "Conflict Resolution and the End of the Cold War, 1989–93." *Journal of Peace Research*. Vol. 31, No. 3, 1994, pp. 333–349.

Baboo, Balgovind; "The Naga National Movement: An Analysis" *Third World Unity*, Vol. 15–16, March–April, 1979, pp. 41–62.

Banerjee, Nirmalya. "Seven Sisters and Big Brother" *The Times of India*, 26 January, 1997.

Banton, M.P.; "Ethnicity, Ethnic Group" in Michael Mann (ed.) *Macmillan Student Encyclopaedia of Sociology*, Macmillan, London, 1983.

Baruah, Banita; "India's Step-Children". *The Times of India*, 26 January, 1997.

Basu Pradip, "The Naga Problem: An Overview", *Asian Studies* 6(2), 1988, pp. 31–49.

Bizo, Khriebu; "Multiplicity of Ethnic Nations". *Nagaland Post*, 13 January, 1996.

Brown, David; "Ethnic Revival: Perspectives on State and Society", *Third World Quarterly* 11(4) October, 1989, pp. 1–17.

Burman, B.K. Roy; "Dynamics of Insurgency in North-East"., *Mainstream*, pp. 15–17., Vol. XXXIII, No. 38, 9 August, 1997.

Carment, David and James, Patrick; "International Constraints and Inter-State Ethnic Conflict, (Toward a Crisis-Based Assessment of Irredentism) *Journal of Conflict Resolution*, Vol. 39, No. 1, March, 1995, pp. 82–109.

Carment, David; "The Ethnic Dimension in World Politics: Theory, Policy and Early Warnings", *Third World Quarterly*, Vol. 15, No. 4, 1994, pp. 551–579.

——: "The International Dimension of Ethnic Conflict: Concepts, Indicators and Theory", *Journal of Peace Research*, Vol. 30, No. 2, 1993, pp. 137–149.

Chakrabarti, Ashis; "Government for Talks Abroad: Nagas" (Muivah Faction Claims 3-Points Consensus), *The Telegraph*, 22 March, 1997.

Chandola, Harish; "Nagaland Cease-fire and Isak Swu" *Mainstream*, Vol. XXXV, No. 35, 9 August, 1997, pp. 6, 38–39.

Chinai, Rupa; "NSCN runs Parallel Government, In North-East, (Helpless administration fails to capitalise on public opinion against insurgents) *The Times of India*, Bombay, 21 January, 1995.

Chowdhury, Suvendu Roy; "People are For Peace", *North-East Sun*, 1–14 July, 1996, p. 8.

——: "Picking Up the Peace", *North-East Sun*, 1–14 July, 1996, pp. 6–7.

——: "What ails Nagaland?" *Northeast Sun*, 25–31 March, 1995, p. 12.

Chowdhury, Rajib; "Is it a Force?: Dotted with Graves of Collapsed Accords the North-East is wary of 'Political Accordism' ", *North-East Sun*, April 1–14, 1997, p. 11.

Clay, Jason W.; "Ethnic Future of Nations." *Third World Quarterly*, Vol. II, No. 4, Oct. 1989, pp. 223–234.

Cooper, Robert and Berdal Mats; "Outside Intervention in Ethnic Conflicts" *Survival*, Vol. 35, No. I, Spring, 1993, pp. 118–142.

D. Nekong, Tongmeth; (Kilonser, Religious Affairs), "Statement (Split up NSCN)", *Nagaland Post*, 2 December, 1996.

Danda, Ajit K.; "Ethnicity and Social Transformation in North-East India" *Man in India* Vol. 72, No. 2, June, 1992, pp. 131–140.

Dasgupta, J.; (cited in Jytorindra Dasgupta), "Community, Authencity and Autonomy: Insurgency and Institutional Development in India's North-East". *The Journal of Asian Studies*, Vol. 56, No. 2, May 1997, p. 355.

Dev, Nirendra: "Nagaland-Myanmar Business", *Nagaland Post*, 7 May, 1996.

Dewan, Deepak; ("Exclusive interview with Naga leaders") Time for peace, part II, *Northeast Sun*, 15–30 September, 1997, pp. 12–16.

Ethnicity and Social Transformation; "Ethnicity in World Politics." *Third World Quarterly* Vol. II, No. 4, Oct. 1989, pp. 1–234 (Series of Articles).

Excerpts from an interview with Gurmukh Singh: "No Compromise on India's Unity." *The Times of India*, 19 May, 1997.

Firoze, Jajansher; "Shadow of Uncertainty", *Northeast Sun*, February, 1–14, 1998, p. 14.

Forty-Third Anniversary of Naga Plebiscite Day." *Nagaland Times*, 17 May, 1994.

Franda, Marcus F.; "The Naga National Council: Origins of a Separatist Movement." *The Economic Weekly Annual*, 4 February, 1961, pp. 153–156.

Furer Haimendorf, C.V.; "Through the Unexplored Mountain of the Assam Burma Border" *Geographical Journal*, Vol. 91, March 1938, pp. 201–219.

G.P.D.; "Beyond the Border Dispute", *Economic and Political Weekly*, p. 1875, 22 October, 1983.

Gabriel, D. Wangsu; "Call for the Naga Unity: Recommendation of the Seventh Session of the 16 General Conference of the NSF, at Phek town. *Northeast Sun*, 11–17 March, 1995, p. 18.

Galtung, Johan; "Future Wars will be more Ethnic and Bloody", *The Pioneer*, 9 October, 1995.

Ganguly, Sumit; "Ethno Religious Conflict in South Asia", *Survival*, Vol. 35, No. 2, Summer 1993, pp. 66–87.

Ghosh, Manosh; "PMO in Dilemma Over NSCN Move." *The Statesman*, 23 February, 1997.

Ghosh, Santanu; "Peace Moves." (The NSCN has responded to the PM's offer for unconditional talks.) Sunday, 24–30 November, 1996, pp. 60–61.

Ghosh, Subir; "Doubts over talks with Naga militants", (Part-II) *The Telegraph*, 20 March, 1997.

——: "History Clouds Prospects of Peace Talks" (Part-I) *The Telegraph*, 21 March, 1997.

——: "Inter-tribe Unity Remains Illusive", (Part-IV) *The Telegraph*, 26 March, 1997.

——: "Militants in no mood to give up Naga Cause". *The Telegraph*, 13 October, 1996.

——: "Nagas to Form Common Platform Soon," (Part-V) *The Telegraph*, 30 March, 1997.

Gokhale, Nitin A.; "The NSCN's Liar, (An outlook team gets a rear behind the scenes glimpse of the Khaplang groups activities)" *Outlook*, 1 December, 1997, pp. 37–39.

Gupta, Barun Das; Will peace get a chance? *The Telegraph*, 27 July, 1997.

Gupta, Barun Das; "Difficult task Ahead", (for a settlement in Nagaland.) *Frontline*, 25 July, 1997, p. 37.

Hadow, E.M.; "Our Raid into Nagaland', *World Wide Magazine*, Feb., 1900.

Hassner, Pierre; "Beyond Nationalism and Internationalism: Ethnicity and World Order", *Survival* Vol. 35, No. 2, Summer, 1993, pp. 49–65.

Hazarika Sanjoy; "Press for Truth", *The Telegraph*, 24 September, 1996, Calcutta.

Hungyo, R.; (President, Tangkhul Hoho Naga). "Tangkhul Naga Hoho on Unity", *Nagaland Post*, 21 February, 1997.

Inside the Forbidden Camp" *Northeast Sun*, 15–31, March, 1998, pp. 17–23.

Insurgency in North-East." *Pylon*, 4–10 September, 1992.

Iralu, Niketu; "Naga Political Movement vis-a-vis Nagas Today". *Nagaland Post*, 6–7 March 1997.

Jami Lotha, A.Z.; (Deputy Kilonser, Ministry of Law & Justice, GPRN) "Naga Political Movement & Present Trauma", *Nagaland Post*, 10 February, 1997.

Jamir, Medem; (Deputy Kilonser, Ministry of Chaplee, NSCN) "Indian and Myanmarese Occupation of Nagaland", *Nagaland Post,* 1 March, 1997.

Jayal, Niraja Gopal; Ethnic diversity and the Nation State, *Journal of Applied philosophy,* Vol. 10, No. 2, 1993. pp. 147–153.

Join, Hand; "*Northeast Sun*", 1–7 August, 1992.

Joint Slaughtering Policy Condemned" (Secretary, MIP, NSCN (GPRN). *Nagaland Post,* 20 June, 1997.

Joute, Joseph; "Is this a Breakthrough ?" *Northeast Sun,* 1–14, April, 1997, p. 30.

Kaping, Apok; "Nagas: The Past, Present and the Future". *Nagaland Post,* 11 December, 1995.

Kaviraj, Sudipta; "Crises of the Nation-State in India", *Political Studies,* Blackwell: Oxford Publication, Vol. XLII, pp. 115–129.

Kent, Rev. Merhupfu; (President, Naga National Council), "The Naga Political Problem", *The Nagaland Journal,* Kohima, Nagaland, 29 May, 1996.

Kiamnungam, P. Pashum; "Partition in Eastern Nagaland", *Nagaland Post,* 3–5, January, 1997.

Kholi, Atul; "Can Democracies Accommodate Ethnic Nationalist: Rise and Fall of Self Determination Movement in India", *Journal of Asian Studies,* Vol. 56, No. 2, May 1997, pp. 342–43.

Laithangbam, Ihoyaima; "Bordering on Trouble." *Rashtriya Sahara,* February, 1996, pp. 60–61.

Lama, J.B.; "Promises Yes, Not Pie Crust", *The Statesman,* 30 October, 1996, Delhi.

Lambert, E.J.D.; "From the Brahmaputra to the Chindwin" *Geographical Journal,* April, 1937.

Lhoursa, Zapuvisie; (President, Angami Regional Council, NNC) Nagas are on the right path, *The Nagaland Journal,* Kohima, Nagaland, 15 March, 1995.

Lucky, K. Mughato; "For Peace and Prosperity", *Northeast Sun,* 1–14 April, 1998, p. 28.

Lungalang, A.K.; (Deputy Kilonser, Ministry of NGO's and Education GPRN) "An advice from a 70 years old Naga Patriot." *Nagaland Post,* 31 January, 1997.

Luthra, Pran Nath; "The Foreign Hand", *The Pioneer,* 28 November, 1997.

——: "The North-East Council, will it prove equal to the task?" *The Statesman,* 24 March, 1997.

Mahapatra, Richard, Lt. Gen. V.K. Nayar; "Alienation Not Insurgency", *Northeast Sun,* 1–14 April, p. 11.

——: "The Peace Offensive", *Northeast Sun,* 1–14 April, 1997, p. 8.

Maj. Gen. Banerjee. D.; "Provoking on Arms Race in South Asia", *The Pioneer,* 10 October, 1995.

Mannerplaw/Subir Bhaumik; "Never Say Die, the (NSCN) Consolidates its Bases in Myanmar", Sunday 16–22 June, 1996.

——: (interviewed Th. Muivah)"Nagas cannot be Crushed by Military Might", *Sunday,* 16–22 June, 1996, pp. 48–52.

Mariang, Angnaikham; (Deputy Kilonser, Ministry of Chaplee, GPRN). "The Martial Law and the Emergence of the NSCN." *Nagaland Post,* 6 March, 1997.

Means, Gordon P. and Means, Ingunn, N.; "The Agony of Ending a Guerrilla War", *Pacific Affairs,* Vol. 39, No. 3&4, Fall and Winter, 1966–67.

Mehta, Maj. Gen. Ashok, K.; "Growing Threat of North-Eastern Rebels". *Hindustan Times,* 23 January, 1997.

Memorandum of Naga Hills. 10 January, 1929. Original letter dated. 26.3.28.

"Militant Outfits of N-E Region in Disarray", *Eastern Clarion,* Silchar, 21–22, August, 1992.

Mitra, Ashok; "Seven Blunders of India." (The military and market economics are leading the North-East to the brink of secession) *The Telegraph,* 16 October, 1996.

Mitra, Debashi; "Insurgents LTTE Links Ominous for North-East". *The Stateman,* 17 April, 1995.

——: "So Sadly Lost in Naivete." *The Statesman,* 6 March, 1997.

——: "The Ball is in Delhi's Court." *The Statesman,* 19 July, 1997.

——: "The Senselessness of it All", *The Statesman.* 29 April, 1997.

——: "Cry a Beloved Country". *The Statesman,* 28 February, 1997.

Naga Territorial Integrity Verses Manipur Territorial Integrity, *The Naga Voice, Kohima,* Nagaland, 3 January, 1997.

Naga Insurgent's Talk Offer ' Mysterious' "*The Assam Tribune* 15 March, 1997.

Naga peace talks (Staff Report): " 'Outsiders' Stall Negotiations", *The Statesman*, 30 March, 1997.

Nagaland Needs Peace (Editorial Column), *The Telegraph*, 29 July, 1997.

Nagas Pledge to Work for Unity at Atlanta Meet, 5 August, *The Statesman*, 1997.

Nayar, Kuldip; "Between the Lines: Britain Sows Seed of Separation." *Nagaland Post*, 1 March, 1997.

Neglect of North-East will increase insurgency (Staff Report): *The Telegraph*, 18 July, 1997.

Nokdenremba, K.; (President, Kohima Ao Senden). "Why Naga Destiny Scours", *Nagaland Post*, 19 February, 1997.

NSCN (I.M.) Rules Out-Talks. (Rivals Presence at Atlanta Meet Irks Isak-Muivah) *The Telegraph*, 23 July, 1997.

NSCN (I.M.) Spurns Jamir Mediation Offer (Staff Report): *The Telegraph*, 18 July, 1997.

NSCN (I.M.) Not to Attend Atlanta Meet." *The Telegraph*, 17 July, 1997.

NSCN Sets Conditions for Talks. *Nagaland Post*, 3 January, 1997.

NSCN's Response to Talks. *Nagaland Post*, 9 June, 1997.

Nuh, Rev. Dr. V.K.; "Sovereignty and Human Right", *Nagaland Post*, 8 December, 1995.

Oinam, Sunil; "North-East Insurgency, Another Front. (Secretary Th. Muivah as the Convenor a new front Self Defence United Front of the South East Himalayan Region has been formed. Comprising of Seven Underground Outfits, The New Front is expected to launch major offensives in the near future) *North-East Sun*, Jan, 14–20, 1995, p. 12.

Oken, Jeet; "Naga Hoho Resolutions", *Northeast Sun*, 1–14 April, 1998, p.14.

Operating in the State. *Northeast Sun*, July 1–14 1996, p. 7.

Pamei, M.K.; (Deputy Kilo Kilonser, Ministry of Kilo Affairs, GPRN). "British Partial occupation of Nagaland." *Nagaland Post*, 27 Februry, 1997.

Pareek, Pradeep; "Peace before Polls". (The NSCN (I.M.) and the Naga intelligentsia say no to elections in Nagaland. *Sunday*, 4–10 January, pp. 46–47.

——: "Give Peace no Chance (A solution to the Naga problem remains elusive.)"*Sunday,* 31 August to 6 September 1997, pp. 61–62.

Patterson, G.N.; "The Naga Problem" *Journal of the Royal Central Asian Society,* Vol. 50, 1963.

——: "Delhi and Nagas" *Far Eastern Economic Review,* 19 May, 1996, pp. 332–334.

Phizo: The Tragic Twist, *Frontline,* 9–22, June, 1990.

Posen Barry R.; "The Security Dilemma and Ethnic Conflict", *Survival,* Vol. 35. No. 1, Spring, 1993, pp. 27–47.

R. Prasannan, "Watching the Nagas (The Meitei are Disturbed at the Prospect of a regrouping of Naga factions, Whose Goal is a Greater Nagaland. Prime Minister evasiveness only adds to fears of division of their state)" *The Week,* 27 July, 1997, pp. 8–10.

Raina, Jay; "Naga Manipur Ultras "Ready" for Talks". *Hindustan Times,* 9 February, 1997.

Rao, not Deve Gowda, First Talked to Naga Rebels." *The Times of India,* 13 April, 1997.

Raveena, "(Insurgency in Nagaland) Following are the Brief Sketches of Major Insurgent Outfits", *North-East Sun,* 1–14 July, 1996.

——: "Anatomy of Insurgency", *North-East Sun,* 29 July, 1998, p. 16–17.

——: "Time For Truce", *North-East Sun,* 1–14, April, 1997, pp. 12–13.

Ray, Tapas; "Fears in Manipur." *Frontline,* 18 April, 1997, pp. 46–48.

——: "Looking for Peace, ('Deve Gowda's initiative has some way to go') *Frontline,* 18 April, 1997, pp. 44–45.

Rebel with a Cause (Editorial), *The Telegraph,* 6 March, 1997.

Reid, Sir Robert; "Assam and the War" *Asiatic Review,* 440 (Jan. 1944) pp. 43–45.

Riggs, Fred W.; "Ethnonationalism, Industrialism, and the Modern State." *Third World Quarterly,* Vol. 15, No. 4, 1994.

Rival Groups Flays NSCN (I.M.) (Correspondent Report), *The Telegraph.* 19 May 1997.

Roy, Ash Narain; "At War With Itself". *The Hindustan Times,* 7 March, 1997.

"Insurgency Movement in North-Eastern India", *Journal of Peace Studies,* Vol. II, Issue 11, July–August, 1995, pp. 205–32.

Ryan, Stephen; "Ethnic Conflict and the United Nations", *Ethnic and Racial Studies,* Vol. 13, No. 1, January, 1990, pp. 25–49.

Seely, John; "History is Past Politics and Politics Presents History: A Political History". *Nagaland Post,* 2 December, 1996.

Sen, D.M.; "Commission report, Army in Nagaland" *Economic and political Weekly,* p. 2284, 2285 and 2287. Vol. XXXI; No. 34, 24–31 August, 1996.

Sen, Kranti; "Spotlight on Nagaland-II Division within the Underground", *Mainstream,* 6 January, 1968, pp. 22–23.

——: "Eastern India in Ferment-III: Peking's Shadow over Nagaland", *Mainstream,* 13 April, 1968, pp. 9–10.

Shaiza, Jacob; "Leadership Clash in the National Socialist Council of Nagaland." *Link,* 27 November, 1988, p. 16.

——: "Threat From the Front." *Northeast Sun,* 28 January to 3 February, 1995, pp. 10–11.

——: "Nagas at a Cross Road (Greater Nagaland)" *North-East Sun,* 22–28 April, 1995. p. 5.

——: "Inhumane Approach", *Rashtriya Sahara,* February, 1996, pp. 60–61.

Sharma, Pranay; "Centre-NSCN Talks Next Month." (Gujral to Make Sure that Demand for 'Greater Nagaland' is not "Entertained." *The Telegraph,* 26 July, 1997.

Shepstone, H.J. and Mills, J.P.; "Head Hunters of Burma", *The Scientific American,* November, 1927. Kohli Atul, Can democracies Accommodate Ethnic Nationalism? Rise and decline of self determination movements in India. *The Journal of Asian Studies* 56, No. 2 (May 1997) pp. 325–344.

Shishak, Tuisem A.; "Nagas for Freedom or Civil War." *Nagaland Post,* 21 August, 1995.

Singh, Prakash; "The Quest for Peace in Nagaland", *Hindustan Times,* 18 May, 1998.

Sinha, Ashish; "Insurgency in the North-East", *The Pioneer* (focus) 21 July, 1997.

Smith, Anthony D.; "Chosen Peoples: Why Ethnic Groups Survive", *Ethnic and Racial Studies* Vol. 15, No. 3, July, 1992, pp. 436–456.

——: "Culture, Community and Territory: The Politics of Ethnicity and Nationalism", *International Affairs,* Vol. 72, No. 3, 1989, p. 447.

Shyam, Pas Chana; "Solution to Naga Problem Illusory", *Link,* 3 July, 1988, p. 30.

Subir, Bhaumik, and Pradeep Pareek; "Herculean Task." (Naga rebels find it hard to unite for starting peace talk with the centre) *Sunday,* 20–26 July, 1997, pp. 26–27.

Subir, Bhaumik; "Farewell: Phizo." *Sunday,* 13–19 May, 1990.

Sunil, Oinam; "NSCN, Faction Flays Cease Fire Agreement." ('Statement by Khaplang likely to jeopardise on going efforts to end violence in Nagaland.') *The Statesman,* 30 July, 1997.

Tambiah, Stanley J.; "Ethnic Conflict in the World Today', American Ethnological Society Distinguished Lecture, Vol. 16, No. 2, May, 1989, pp. 335–349.

Temjen, N.; "Nagaland-Qua-vadis". *Nagaland Post,* 6–7 December, 1996.

The Administrator, (Journal of Lal Bahadur Shastri National Academy of Administration, Missouri) Special issue on North-East, Wiley Eastern Limited. New age International Publishers.

The Fourth Naga Hoho Summit (Editorial), *Nagaland Post,* Nagaland, 18 February, 1997.

Th. Muivah; interview by Subir Bhaumik M. "On the Past, Present and Future of the Naga Struggle" (Nagas cannot be crushed by Military might) *Sunday,* 16–22 June, 1996.

The Naga Problem: An Account. Seminar Paper—Jointly Sponsored by Citizens for Democracy and The Naga Students' Federation, New Delhi, 14 December, 1995.

The New Messiah, *Sunday,* 30 December, 1990–5; January, 1991.

The Underground Link, (editorial column) Excerpts from, Jug Suraiya's, "First hand Account of Nagaland", written almost 25 years ago. *The Times of India* 26 January, 1997.

The voice of Northeast "Cautious Optimism." *Northeast Sun,* 1–14 April, 1997, p. 4.

The Yehzabo of Nagaland.

Therie Teisoviknolie, "Naga Political Movement, Crisis & its Affects," *Nagaland Post*, 9 June, 1997.

——: "Naga Political Movement Crisis & its Affects." *Nagaland Post*, 10 June, 1997.

——: "Naga Political Movement: Crisis and its Affects." *Nagaland Post*, 5–7 June, 1997.

Transgressing their Brief," *The Statesman*, 12 December, 1996.

Underground Realities ('Extracts from Chaman Lal's easy disorder to secession on why insurgency continues to plaque the Nation') *Sunday*, 3–9 May, 1998.

Vanessa, Baird; Why do so many new stories never make the news? (examines some of the obstacles in their way.) *New Internationalist*, Spiked! No. 356/June 1994, pp. 4 & 5.

Veyie, Yesonu; (President CPO & Chairmen, NHS, Kohima). "NHS Welcomes UNC's Resolution on Integration - Resolution Adopted by the Naga Hoho Summit in its Meeting Held on 26–27 August 1997 in APO Conference Hall, Kohima. *"The Naga voice"*, Kohima Nagaland, 10 September, 1997.

Walker, Jenonne; "International Mediation of Ethnic Conflicts", *Survival*. Vol. 35, No. 1 Spring 1993, pp. 102–117.

Ward, David; "Nagaland: The Tears behind the Blindfold", *The Nagaland Journal*, Kohima, Nagaland, 15 March, 1995.

Warren, Mercus; "What happened to war?" (The spread of peace pushes wars and conflicts deeper into the third world and farther away from the developed nations) *The Pioneer*, 7 January, 1996.

Weiner, Myron; "Peoples and States in a New Ethnic Order", *Third World Quarterly*, Vol. 13, No. 2, 1997, p. 317.

——: "Sons of the Soil, Migration and Ethnic Complaint in India", Princeton: Princeton University Press, 1978.

Welsh, David; "Domestic Politics and Ethnic Conflict", *Survival*, Vol. 35, No. 1, Spring 1993, pp. 63–80.

Zubaida, Sami; "Nations: Old and New Comments on Anthony D. Smith's "The myth of the 'modern nations' and the Myths of Nations". *Ethnic and Racial Studies*, Vol. 12, No. 3, 3 July, 1989, pp. 329–338.